Be Still and Know

Be Still and Know

Zen and the Bible

Ruben L. F. Habito

ORBIS BOOKS
www.orbisbooks.com

ORBIS BOOKS
Maryknoll, New York 10545
Founded in 1970, Orbis Books endeavors to publish works that enlighten the mind, nourish the spirit, and challenge the conscience. The publishing arm of the Maryknoll Fathers and Brothers, Orbis seeks to explore the global dimensions of the Christian faith and mission, to invite dialogue with diverse cultures and religious traditions, and to serve the cause of reconciliation and peace. The books published reflect the views of their authors and do not represent the official position of the Maryknoll Society. To learn more about Maryknoll and Orbis Books, please visit our website at www.maryknollsociety.org.

Library of Congress Cataloging-in-Publication Data

Names: Habito, Ruben L. F., 1947– author.
Title: Be still and know : Zen and the Bible / Ruben L.F. Habito.
Description: Maryknoll, New York : Orbis Books, [2017] | Includes
   bibliographical references and index.
Identifiers: LCCN 2016042677 (print) | LCCN 2017002176 (ebook) |
   ISBN 9781626982154 (pbk.) | ISBN 9781608336807 (e-book)
Subjects: LCSH: Bible—Meditations. | Christianity and other religions—
   Zen Buddhism. | Zen Buddhism—Relations—Christianity.
Classification: LCC BS491.5 .H33 2017 (print) | LCC BS491.5 (ebook) | DDC
261.2/43927--dc23
LC record available at https://lccn.loc.gov/2016042677

To Maria Kannon, and all that she represents

Contents

Preface . . . .*ix*

Introduction: *A Time of Quiet, a Time of Grace* . . . . *xii*

Chapter One: Be Still and Know
  (Psalm 46) 1
  Our Refuge and Strength in Troubled Times 1
  Overcoming Our Fears 10
  Thirsting and Yearning for Living Waters 19
  Behold in Awe and Wonder 32
  Searching for True Self 39

Chapter Two: My Cup Overflows
  (Psalm 23) 47
  Drawn by an Inner Thirst 47
  Calling on the Unnamable 50
  Finding Belonging in a Spiritual Community 59
  I Know Only Contentment 63
  All the Days of Our Lives 66

Chapter Three: The Treasure That Is You
  (Matthew 13:44–46) 79
  Is That All There Is? 79
  Digging for the Treasure 83
  The Treasure Was There All Along 88
  The Infinite Is Here and Now 100
  Glowing Like the Sun 105

Chapter Four: Blessed Are You
  (Matthew 5:1–3, 8–9) 117
  Blessed 117
  Blessed Are the Poor in Spirit. 126
  The Kin-dom in Our Midst. 138
  Blessed Are the Pure of Heart. 148
  For They Shall See God 159

Conclusion:
  Zen and the Bible: Experiencing a Loving Presence. 169

Appendix: Other Fingers Pointing to the Moon 172

Acknowledgments. 183

Index. 189

Preface

On many occasions during the course of my Zen training in Japan in the 1970s and 1980s, my Zen Master, Yamada Kōun Rōshi, would offer encouraging words to the long-time practitioners who were receiving his one-on-one guidance. "If you are ever put in a situation of being asked to guide others in taking this path of Zen, you yourself must first be immersed in it thoroughly, having plumbed its depths and being thus able to see through the world of Zen from inside out." Then, turning specifically to those of us from a Christian background, he offered a challenge. "The words and ideas you have heard from me to guide you in your Zen practice derive from the Buddhist religious tradition. But as you go back to your communities and they ask you about Zen, learn to use language that your Christian audience may readily understand. You must therefore familiarize yourself with your own Bible and bring out whatever would be effective pointers that you may find there, so they too may experience for themselves the world of Zen, which, as you know, is ultimately beyond all words and concepts."[1]

This book emerged out of talks offered at Zen retreats conducted at Osage Monastery and Forest of Peace in Sand Springs, Oklahoma, over a period of several years. Many of the participants were devout Catholics or Christians from

---

[1] In Zen tradition, a well-known saying is that words and concepts are like "fingers pointing to the moon," the luminous "moon" of Zen enlightenment.

different denominations, together with individuals who may have been raised in Christian surroundings but who had not been attending church for some time; there were also others from assorted religious and nonreligious backgrounds, all seeking to deepen their spiritual life through Zen practice. It was a privilege and joy for me to have been invited by Sister Pascaline Coff, OSB, and the members of the resident Benedictine sisters' community there at Osage, to come as a teacher for those annual retreats for over two decades. The talks and the guidance to individuals I offered at those retreats derived, on the one hand, from what I myself had received from the Zen Buddhist practice I was schooled in for many years in Japan before coming to the United States and, on the other, from the Catholic Christian spirituality I had been nurtured in since my youth in the Philippines and through nearly twenty-five years as a member of the Society of Jesus, most of them spent in Japan.

It was the Spiritual Exercises of Ignatius of Loyola that formed the foundation of my Jesuit life. I began to engage in Zen practice while still in training as a Jesuit, and these two sources continue to be the mainsprings of my spiritual nourishment. I have written about the encounter between Zen and the Spiritual Exercises of Ignatius of Loyola in a previous work, so I will not go into detail about this here and only refer the interested reader to check out that book.[2]

The retreats conducted at Osage turned out to be a marvelous point of intersection between the Zen Buddhist and the Christian traditions, like two different wellsprings of fresh running water coming together at a certain turn of a stream to provide nourishment for all those who come to drink.

---

[2] See Ruben L. F. Habito, *Zen and the Spiritual Exercises: Paths of Awakening and Transformation* (Maryknoll, NY: Orbis Books, 2013).

Some of those talks given during the retreats were fortunately recorded and then transcribed, and I kept these in my files for a while. As I pored over those transcriptions again after some years of having set them aside, the inspiration came to put them together in a volume as a resource for those who, for various reasons, feel a tug from within and are drawn to engage in some form of spiritual practice. If you are such a person, this book is for you.

Introduction:
A Time of Quiet, a Time of Grace

As we continue our busy and hectic lives, every now and then we may feel a tug from within, making us somewhat ill at ease, or perhaps telling us in some way or other, "Slow down! Take a look at yourself. What are you doing? Where are you heading?" Heeding this voice from within and taking it to heart provide the impetus to take a break from our normal schedule, enter into a time of quiet, and give ourselves an opportunity to pause and ponder the big questions of life: What is the point of all this? Where am I heading? What is the meaning of my life?

A spiritual retreat is such a time when one may open oneself to listen more deeply to these stirrings from within. It provides a setting wherein one takes a break from one's normal day-to-day activities and devotes oneself to a time of contemplative silence. It is in this atmosphere that one may be able to reclaim one's grounding in life, arrive at a deeper appreciation of the gifts one has been receiving all along, be opened to new directions, or perhaps experience a transformation of one's total outlook and attitude.

There are passages in the New Testament indicating that Jesus went into retreat time and again. Right before launching his ministry, Jesus goes into the wilderness for forty days and forty nights (Matt. 4:1). In the midst of a life actively engaged in proclaiming God's word to people, "Jesus often withdrew to lonely places and prayed" (Luke 5:16). On a given occasion, having spoken to the crowds, "He dismisses them, and goes up on a mountainside to pray." (Matt. 14:22–23).

Zen Buddhism offers a concrete and methodical way of launching into a spiritual journey, leading to an experience of awakening, unfolding in a life of ongoing transformation. A Zen retreat is called *sesshin,* the Japanese pronunciation of a compound of two Chinese characters, which together mean "to regulate the mind." It is a special time when practitioners devote somewhere between eight and ten hours a day in seated meditation, in addition to practice in silence, walking meditation, listening to a talk, and one-on-one consultations with the teacher on matters of Zen practice, not to mention meals, rest, and taking care of personal needs, all in mindful attention at each moment. *Sesshin* can also be read as meaning "to be touched at the heart," or "encounter of the heart," wherein "heart" refers to the core of one's being, as when we say, "the heart of the matter." As a person enters the silence and is immersed in the stillness, the heart becomes open and is able to "see" things in a radically new way. This is an experiential event called "seeing one's true nature," that is, seeing the truth about oneself and about everything that exists in this whole vast universe. This event can be pivotal in the life of a practitioner, ushering in a new way of seeing and understanding the world, oneself, one's entire life.

In ways that resonate with the above, Jesus speaks of *metanoia,* literally, "changing one's mind," and usually translated as "repentance" or "conversion." This refers to a spiritual event that entails a veritable transformation of one's total outlook and attitude toward oneself and toward life as a whole.

In a Zen retreat, participants are enjoined to maintain strict silence at all times, avoid unnecessary and distracting thoughts (such as planning for the future, daydreaming, etc.) or activities (using the cell phone to read or send text messages), and instead to keep coming back to the *here and now,* whether in meditation, walking, taking meals, doing chores, and so on. The central attitude to be maintained throughout all this is to *pay attention,* in a way in which one is alert and yet at the same time relaxed. This "relaxed attentiveness" is to be maintained throughout the entire day, from the moment one wakes up in the morning to the time one dozes off to sleep at night.

As I look back at the many Zen retreats I have participated in over the past four decades, as a practitioner or assisting as guiding teacher, I can only bow my head in great awe and wonder and gratitude, experiencing firsthand the marvelous and deeply moving things that happen to people during those periods of time spent in silence and in paying attention to what is happening in the present moment. A Christian would refer to these as "times of grace," indeed, times when grace is poured out like rain from the sky, and in torrents at that.

This book comes with an invitation to enter into such a time of quiet, which can also be a profoundly rich time of grace. It is not meant to be read from cover to cover for whatever ideas it may have to offer about Zen or about the Bible, but rather it is offered as something like a menu awaiting the reader who may be disposed to take the time to partake of the feast. What it offers can hopefully be taken as pointers toward a direction that the reader's own inner voice is already urging and leading to, but which he or she may not be able to fully articulate. "Come, taste and see."

Chapter One

Be Still and Know (Psalm 46)

Our Refuge and Strength in Troubled Times

We live in troubled times. This has been true throughout many epochs of human history, but it can certainly be said especially in this twenty-first century of the common era. The media keep calling our attention to events in many places in the world that do not bode well for our human family. Racial issues, not to mention economic disparity, culture wars, and political differences, continue to be sources of tension and discord in what is called the *United* States. Armed violence continues to be a daily occurrence in many regions of the world, perpetrated by individuals and by groups. Millions of people are displaced from their ancestral homes as a result of this armed violence and are driven to become refugees and migrants. Our survival as a species is threatened by an ongoing ecological crisis of global proportions, with impending climate change that will have cataclysmic implications for the entire planet.

If we come to a contemplative retreat with the intention of shutting ourselves off from the rest of the world and finding

1

a haven of peace in a secluded place, so that we can just be content with ourselves and forget everything else, then we misunderstand contemplative practice entirely. In the contemplative life, we do not escape from the world, but rather we follow a path that enables us to plunge right into the heart of the world. A genuinely spiritual person is not one who seeks an escape from the realities of everyday life, but rather one who is able to see these realities with new eyes, with an open heart and mind.

Following the call to live a spiritual life involves entering a path that takes a straightforward gaze at the realities of the world where there is so much suffering, so much violence, so much to lament. And in the middle of all this, our hearts are also drawn to go deeper and look deeper into things, to find a place of peace (*shalom*), a place of *shabbat* (rest). As we are able to discover wherein lies that place of peace in the midst of this violent world, we are able to offer that peace as our gift to the entire world.

In our search for that place of peace, let us look to Psalm 46, for some pointers to help us along the Way.

You are our refuge and our strength,
Help in the storm of anguish and despair
Exactly and easily found close at hand
So we are not afraid.

Even when earth's in upheaval
When mountains are carried to the sea
When the sea's waters roar and foam
And the mountains quake and tremble with the waters' swelling—

In the middle of the world there is a river
Streams run to it, making glad your cities
Making glad the places where you are known

You flow as the waters of that river
And she shall not be moved
For you are with her
You are the morning that dawns over the quiet waters

Nations rage, kingdoms tumble—
This is the sound of your voice
This is the earth melting away
You are with us, our defense, our silent center
What we see is all your doing
These desolations
These terrifying moments—
Only our unmoving movement
You cause wars to cease when they cease, to cease forever
You break the bow, snap the spear
Burn up the war wagons

Be still—be still
And know me
Be still and know
That I am what the nations grope toward
I am the earth's desire
Our defense at the silent center of things.[1]

You are our refuge and our strength.

Unfortunately we look in many other places for refuge, and then we realize that they are *not* where we will find that which we seek.

That we seek refuge is, in itself, an indication that we are in a state of powerlessness, or that we have been displaced

---

[1] Translation is from Norman Fischer, *Opening to You: Zen-Inspired Translations of the Psalms* (New York: Penguin Books, 2003).

from our true homes—"refugees" in the spiritual sense of the word. That word, "refugee," brings forth the images of millions of peoples throughout the world who have been displaced from their homes due to threats of physical violence, due to extremely difficult situations in their lives that threaten their very survival, or else due to dire economic necessity. These events happen to millions of peoples in different parts of the world. Even now, right now, as we sit and enjoy our silence, somewhere families are being driven out of their homes for various reasons.

As we look deeper into our own lives, we realize that we too have been displaced from our true homes, in the sense that we do not yet have the experience of that deep peace that assures us we are at home in this universe. We are dogged by a sense of dissatisfaction, restlessness, a sense of displacement. There is something within us that beckons, "Come home!"

We feel that longing to come home, to seek refuge in a place of peace where we can truly feel at home, at rest, deep in our hearts. So if we are still unable to say to ourselves, "I am at home, right here and now," then this is an invitation for us to consider these questions: "Where is my home? How can I find it? Where can I seek refuge?"

It may be that our own current pursuits, those things that occupy our time and energy from day to day, and also the very things we try to hold onto for some kind of satisfaction or comfort, are the very things that give us this inner sense of uprootedness and restlessness, of not being "at home" with ourselves.

As we look at our global society, especially through the lens of the so-called industrialized world, we see an abundance of material goods dangled before our eyes by the mass media, enticing us, telling us that we must have this or we need that, in order to feel happy and satisfied with ourselves. People are driven to feel the need to possess different things in their lives to give themselves that sense of self-satisfaction. For example, we find ourselves in continual search for new thrills and new pleasures. The entertainment industry keeps coming up with new attractions, one after another, and so we gladly buy into these. We want to be up to date on the latest fads, the latest movies, the latest video games, the newest car model, the latest version of iPhone. There is always that drive to want more, to have more.

As we consider what happens in the process, we realize that the more "stuff" we buy, the deeper we go into a state of dissatisfaction. If we cannot acquire the things we think we want, we get frustrated. If we do get to be one of those lucky ones to have enough means and get what we want, still somehow we are left with that sense of dissatisfaction, of lack of fulfillment, leading us ask ourselves, "Really, is that all there is?"

As we are propelled by our inner need to secure our place in the world, we seek more possessions, to give us a sense of "power" over more things. We want more in our bank account. We want a bigger house; we want a flashier car. We want more satisfying relationships. We want to have all of those good things the "cool people" in society seem to have. Of course! Who doesn't? And so we are driven to work more, to strive more, to keep pumping the gas of our inner accelerator. As we do, the more we are engulfed by a sense of powerlessness, and we are thrown even further away from that sense of being truly at home with the universe, at home within ourselves.

This external force of wanting more drives us to be more successful, to be more powerful. That desire to be more powerful is a dynamism that drives not only individuals like us, but also social groups, corporations, political parties, governments, nation-states, and so on. The drive for power, be it in an individual or particular group, will inevitably lead us to clash with others who also want power. This results in the kind of world we live in, namely, a world of conflict, violence, warfare, and enmity between human beings on different levels.

We bring about this kind of world by our own misplaced search for power and possessions, and we only aggravate our own misery as we continue this pursuit, being confused and not knowing wherein our true satisfaction lies. If you think that your satisfaction will depend on getting that bigger house or getting a bigger salary, acquiring more perks at work, putting more stuff in your house, or getting elevated to a higher status in society, and all that, then go ahead, go for it. Do all you can to achieve this, and see what happens. And when you *do* come to realize that *that* way of going about life is not where true satisfaction can be found, as many earnest individuals inevitably come to realize at some point in their lives, then you are ready to hear the message of this psalm.

You are our refuge and our strength. This is what Augustine of Hippo came to realize, after years of giving himself to various pursuits, including sex, fame, power, and prestige, and the like. He is finally led to exclaim, from the depths of his heart, that utterance that resonates through centuries of our human history: *"Our hearts are restless until they rest in You."* This You that Augustine addresses is the same You that our psalm points us toward. *"You are our refuge and our strength."*

The Latin for the English word translated as "restless" is *inquietum est*, captured better in the Spanish word *inquietud,* a state of inner un-ease, dis-ease. This "dis-ease" (*dukkha*) is what Siddhartha Gautama saw and felt most deeply as he looked at his own life in the palace, which led him to make the Great Resolve to launch out into the world, seeking for the truth about our human condition.

This is the same state of un-ease, of restlessness, that led the Second Chan (Zen) Ancestor in China (Dazu Huike, Jp.

Taiso Eka, 487–593) to seek counsel, and guidance from the Bodhidharma, handed down to us in the famous encounter that brought Chan/Zen to open new horizons in China.

> *"Master, my mind is not at peace. Please give it rest." (Gateless Gate, No. 42)*

After a search that took six years, Siddhartha arrived at a place of peace as he sat under the bodhi tree. The Second Ancestor arrived at it through sitting in stillness, receiving the guidance of the sage Bodhidharma. Augustine arrived at his place of rest, entrusting himself entirely to the You that he addresses in his prayer. We are invited to join Siddhartha, the Second Ancestor, and Augustine, and countless others in our human history who embarked on a spiritual quest, to plumb the depths of that place of rest that Augustine refers to here, the same place that the psalmist attests to in proclaiming, *"You are our refuge and our strength."* We will look into this more closely and in detail as we go along.

What is meant by "refuge"? Let us look into this, taking a tour through a Buddhist path. In this tradition, one who seeks to live the path of awakening begins by proclaiming oneself as taking refuge in the Three Jewels.

> *I take refuge in Buddha.*
> *I take refuge in Dharma.*
> *I take refuge in Sangha.*

I take refuge in the Buddha, the Awakened One. When one says "I take refuge in the Buddha," one expresses an aspiration toward living a life that is awakened. The experience of awakening enables us to see through the causes of our dissatisfaction and thus to be empowered to overcome them, to be liberated from them. This awakening can bring deep inner peace in our lives and thus unleash the powers of compassion latent within our own being. To take refuge in the Awakened One, and in awakening itself, is simply to align my life in the direction of all that would lead me to the place of peace, and thus live a life of wisdom and compassion.

I take refuge in the *dharma*, the liberating truth realized by all awakened ones. In simple terms, this means that my refuge will be in reality itself, freed from all delusions: the truth of "what is, and all that there is," nothing more and nothing less. In taking refuge in the dharma, we place ourselves in that direction of living in the light of truth, and align our lives so that we may be able to see "what truly is," and face up to reality face to face, as it were. We direct ourselves so that we are not sidetracked by delusions or disordered affections, nor by the misleading images and values that are thrown in our path by the media or by our culture. We see things as they are with clarity and inner freedom, in a way that liberates us. "The truth shall make you free," as John 8:32 affirms.

I take refuge in the *Sangha*, in the community that will support me in this path of awakening. If we look at those around us, we will find the *sangha* we are looking for, that community of beings with whom we seek awakening together. I am often told during my retreats by participants how sitting together with a group truly gives a new kind of energy to them. It not only perks us up in our own contemplative practice, but it also gives us a deeper sense of connectedness with those around us, and with the entire world as well. Whenever we sit together as *sangha*, we embrace the opportunity of sitting together in silence in community with those who are on the same path. This can be greatly transformative for each and every one of us. So we express our gratitude to each and every one around us for their being our *sangha,* our community, or better, family of spiritual support. We take refuge in one another, in that sense.

To summarize, first, it is awakening itself; second, it is the reality that everyone awakens to; and third, the community of those seeking that awakening collectively—these three are "our refuge and our strength."

The psalmist counsels us: Do not to seek refuge in those finite things that pass away, things that will inevitably betray you or leave you unsatisfied. Instead, seek refuge in that which is truly solid and immovable and steadfast, and yet readily accessible here and now, "an ever-present help in distress."

We need to ask ourselves as we go through this life: In fact, where are we seeking refuge? We need to examine our lives and see whether we cling to temporary or impermanent things that will eventually vanish or fade away, and come to the realization that they are not worth seeking as refuge. We are called to seek refuge in that which is, that which is infinite and timeless, that which is boundless, that which is ever-present right here and now. This mode of contemplative practice that we are taught in Zen, which consists in simply sitting and breathing in and out, and letting our minds rest in the here and now, enables us to find the true place of refuge.

For now, let us jump ahead to the end of the psalm: *Be still and know. . . .* Be still. The invitation for us then is simply that, be still, maintain that stillness and there you will find all that you seek: the fullness of being, full awareness, and unmitigated bliss. In this stillness, let us take refuge, and dwell therein.

You are our refuge and our strength,
Help in the storm of anguish and despair
Exactly and easily found close at hand.

In that stillness, we are able to place ourselves at the eye of the storm, as it were, and be able to live through the turmoil of our lives, look squarely in the eye at the anguish and despair that may be impinging on us, that seems to be threatening us, and not be perturbed, for we know the source of true inner peace. It is not something we need to look for anywhere else than where we already are, right here, right now, so close at hand. Just be still, and you will know.

Overcoming Our Fears

So we are not afraid.
Even when earth's in upheaval
When mountains are carried to the sea
When the sea's waters roar and foam
And the mountains quake and tremble with the waters' swelling—

Fear prevents us from finding our true home. We need to examine the roots of fear in our lives. Sometimes people who come to a deeper state of contemplative practice tend to be thrown off because when they are there in the depths, they realize that their conventional securities are being taken away. They become afraid. They say, "I don't want to do that. I don't know where I am going." Rather than going forward, we may tend to recoil and hang back grabbing hold of those things with which we are more familiar. That can hinder us from arriving at the place of peace.

The psalmist encourages us: Fear not! The other word that is behind that "fear not" is simply, "Trust!" Trust that you are in good hands. Trust that you are being embraced by something that affirms you and upholds you and seeks the fullness of your well-being. Trust that you are in the right place. Trust that you are accepted just as you are. Let go of all those things that prevent you from taking a free fall and giving your whole being to the big unknown, the big mystery calling you right here and now in this stillness.

For those of you who have been in this practice for some time now, you may have moved beyond those distractions or diversions. You are no longer clinging to those thrills, or propelled by a drive for power, or driven by some external impulse you are not fully conscious of. You see that you are already deeper on the path, but this is where we may need to check anew what hinders us from going deeper. There may be that fear, the fear that in venturing to the unknown, you will lose everything that you have already attained for yourselves, and so you recoil and are tempted to turn back. Here we are enjoined; "Fear not, Just trust that you are in good hands, and go on forward, deeper into the Mystery."

What are those conventional securities that we are asked to let go of? One of the things that can help us is to look at the Three Marks of Dharma as taught by the Buddha, the three indications of what that reality is to which we are called to awaken. What are these?

These three marks of the dharma, or facets of reality, as pointed out to us by the Awakened One are impermanence, unsatisfactoriness, and not-self. As we begin to recognize these on the surface level as applying to our own lives, these marks can generate fear within us. But a deeper look at them, looking at each of them "straight in the eye," as it were, is what enables us to overcome that fear.

When we harbor the delusion that our life is going to continue just the way it has been, that it is going to be just as we have always experienced it, the mark of impermanence may begin to knock on our door at any point. When it does, through some "interrupt" that thwarts us from our regular pace of life, like the loss of a job, the loss of a loved one, a diagnosis of a terminal illness, or some other kind of "bolt out of the blue" that knocks us out of balance, we come to realize that nothing on this earth, in this humdrum world of phenomena that we take for granted in our lives from day to day, will remain steadfast as it is, in the way we may want things to be. We come to realize that those things we have been banking on will all be passing anyway, that we will eventually lose our hold of them. This initial sense of impermanence may feel threatening to our entire project of life as we knew it up to that point, so we begin to feel insecure and fearful.

This is where the Awakened One invites us to look more deeply into the fact of impermanence. Because things do pass away and are not permanent, we can now see that each moment of our life is just like that, "just as it is." It is an invitation to live this life of impermanence from moment to moment and find a sense therein of acceptance and be at peace with it. Rather than expound further on this, I would like to invite us all just to be still in the present moment and try to catch but not hold onto a thought, an experience, and an idea. I invite you simply to take each moment in the way it is. The next moment may be entirely different, but this moment is something that we can now accept the way it is, and so on with the next moment.

Consider the simple act of walking. If we can walk in a way that enables us to experience each step, and be able to take each step with trust, knowing that the earth is there to support us, then with each step we know we are in good hands. We take the next step, and the next, with the same full presence there. If we take a broad angle view of this act of walking, we will notice that with every step, we are actually taking a risk of falling off balance in lifting one foot, and then another, and that our body moves its center of gravity moment after moment as we do so. And yet it is our trust that we are held firmly by the ground beneath us that enables us to walk at ease and not feel insecure each time. Considering this act of walking serves as an invitation to live impermanence in each moment, with trust. In so doing, we find our source of refuge in each present moment, and not in the thought that "this will continue on and on." We are invited to live that impermanent moment, and find eternity within it, an eternal now, a place of peace, from which to see through impermanence and live in the fullness of each present moment.

We experience a feeling of dissatisfaction when we pursue finite things that tend to elude our grasp. The drivenness with which we pursue things may pump up our juices and make us feel excited and exert our efforts toward acquiring what we desire, whether material gain or intellectual accomplishment, or even a spiritual benefit. And then, if we are fortunate in actually being able to acquire what we had sought, the moment it comes into our possession, this excitement subsides, and then we turn our mind in another direction and begin to pursue something else. This is a signal for us that as long as we continue to live in this flow of life that goes from past to present to an ongoing and unknown future, we will always feel incomplete, and there is something deep in us that remains unsatisfied and can never be totally quenched in this finite and mortal life of ours.

In realizing this, we feel the need to look more deeply in our lives and thus find the motivation to begin some form of spiritual practice. As we go on further and deeper in our experience of contemplative practice, we will be enabled to see through those things with which we have been unsatisfied, and clearly see them as such. Again this resonates with what Saint Augustine noted, as he exclaimed, "Our hearts are restless until they rest in You." We realize that these finite pursuits that tended to occupy us and make us anxious are things that will ultimately not give us satisfaction. This realization can give us the inner freedom to let go of them, and turn our hearts to something more important, more deeply satisfying.

In this connection, I am reminded of the film *As Good as It Gets*, starring Helen Hunt and Jack Nicholson. The plot is too complicated to summarize here, but the message I receive from the film is as follows: If we have high expectations of life, of an idealized partner, or idealized situations, we are always frustrated. We do not realize that what we are really seeking, that which will give us true contentment and happiness, is right there in front of us, in our very midst. We cannot see it, however, because we are always idealizing, expecting something else, something "better" or "more sublime." Beyond the pockmarks, beyond the sharp edges, beyond the fumbling and struggling, in short beyond the imperfectness of human beings who are just being themselves, we may at some moment come to realize that we are okay just the way we are, warts and all. Then perhaps we can realize that in that very "unsatisfactoriness" that leaves our hearts longing for something more, we can find a sense of acceptance, and thereby of peace, and become truly grateful for things just the way they are.

To see through that unsatisfactoriness in a way that can overcome our fear is to hear that cosmic affirmation that we are accepted just as we are. We participate in the fullness of being just as we are, with our limitations and weaknesses. To see and *to accept* those limitations of ourselves and also of those around us, beyond all our idealizations and high expectations, can also enable us to overcome that sense of dissatisfaction we find as we look at others and want something other than what they really are.

Another aspect of reality taught by the Awakened One pertains to the desire to identify with something that can give us our foothold, a sense of our place, and a sense of ourselves in this world. Unwittingly, influenced by what we see and hear and feel from how those around us relate to us or perceive us, or what they convey to us, we form a construct of an idealized "self" that would secure our own place and identity vis-à-vis others. This third aspect of reality tells us that those ideas that we have construed of our own self and of our own identity are precisely that—our own constructs. Our True Self, in contrast, is in a realm we can discover only as we let go of that constructed self that we think or imagine we are. It is this constructed, and therefore delusive, self that continues to pursue those impermanent and ultimately unsatisfactory things to which we tend to cling. Only when we let go of this constructed, idealized self and let go of the clinging associated with it will we be able to arrive at a place that enables us to be at home in the universe, that gives us true inner peace.

This second line of the psalm, "We fear not, though the earth be shaken and mountains plunge into the depths of the sea," is an invitation for us. Fear not letting go of those idealizations, conventional securities, and identifications of self; instead, just stay there and trust that you are accepted just as you are. In that place of trust, we are now able to go deeper. And how do we go deeper?

Be still, and know me.

In that stillness, we will know. Who is this "me" (in Norman Fischer's translation) that we will "know" in that stillness? The usual translation for this passage would be, "Be still, and know that I am God." We will look at this later, putting this on hold for now. Let us just allow the stillness to reverberate throughout our being and continue sitting in silence.

Even when the earth is in upheaval
When mountains are carried out into the sea
When the sea's waters roar and foam
And the mountains quake and tremble with the waters' flowing
. . . You are with us, our defense, our silent center.

Taking the NRSV translation of the psalm also offers an angle.

The nations are in an uproar, the kingdoms totter;
he utters his voice, the earth melts.
The LORD *of hosts is with us; the God of Jacob is our refuge.*

"The God of Jacob is our refuge." What is the significance for us of this reference to the "God of Jacob"? We recall the passage in Genesis (32:22–32) wherein Jacob, son of Isaac, son of Abraham, encountered the Holy, in a wrestling match. Perhaps this indicates that we are also called to engage in a wrestling match. The practice of sitting in stillness, paying attention to the breath, allowing the mind to come to focus in the here and now, can be precisely that, a wrestling match. There may still be many things in our lives that we still need to wrestle with: our attachments, our fears, our illusions or delusions, and so on. As we wrestle with them, we realize that we have been placing those obstacles in our path all along. As we wrestle with them, we realize the only way is to let go.

The psalmist invokes the God of Jacob, inviting us to recall that image of Jacob wrestling with God, reminding us of our own wrestling match within ourselves, with all that prevents us from finding inner peace, joy, security, our true home—whatever those may be in particular for each of us. These would include elements arising out of the three poisons of greed, anger, and ignorance. These could be our insecurities, misgivings, resentments, and ill will toward those whom we regard as enemies or threats to our well-being. These could include our clinging to our own self-image and our delusions in a way that hampers our freedom to accept ourselves just as we are.

Whatever it is that prevents us from becoming fully ourselves, from realizing that peace for which our heart and our whole being yearn, that is what we need to wrestle with. Sitting in stillness, observing with equanimity those things that prevent us from becoming fully ourselves may allow us to make those things simply melt away, so that we can surrender, so that we may experience the freedom to simply accept ourselves, *just as we are.*

The image of the God of Jacob in Psalm 46 is a guide for us, inviting us to recognize those issues that we need to wrestle with in our lives. For now, let us take this "God of Jacob" as a placeholder for that Holy, Mysterious One that we yearn for and long for deep in our hearts. To wrestle with the God of Jacob is to realize that there is no way we can get through this with our own little puny selves, to realize that we are overpowered, and that all we need to do is surrender. We are told: Fear not, trust, and surrender—I AM *an ever-present help in time of distress.*

So, sitting still, as the mind goes off here and there, let us simply keep coming back to the here and now. Just breathe in and breathe out. Experience the stillness, and in that stillness you will find what you are looking for. In that stillness, you will arrive at the place of peace. At that place of peace, you will also see how we are connected with all beings, who are also seeking peace like ourselves. From that place of peace, we will also come to know how we may be a gift of peace to one another and to the rest of the world.

Before we can put out the fires going on in the world, we must first put out the fire in ourselves that rages and blocks our inner peace. Let us continue to come back to that stillness and simply taste each present moment.

It is not just in the sitting that we are invited to come back to the ever-present moment. The sitting, of course, is the most intense time when we can taste that invitation, but during our walks, our meals, our chores, and all our daily living, we receive the invitation to find, here and now, that for which we are looking. When we accept that invitation, we are able to come home. That is our refuge. In the here and now, we will find our true refuge. And so let us come back to that home together.

We are invited to be still, and lo and behold, everything we are looking for in our lives, in our spiritual paths, can be found as we deepen our immersion and dwell in that stillness. This is a hint, or a roadmap, we could say. It sets a path for us that is really no path, because, we will discover as we move along this path, that we have been there right from the start. Perhaps we only know this in varying degrees, or perhaps we do not know it at all yet.

The core message of Psalm 46, is translated in English as "*Be still and know that I am God.*" Another translation renders this verse like this: "Desist (from your useless striving and clinging and trying to get the better of the situation), and confess that I am God." Reading the Hebrew, if one might translate this loosely, it is something like, "Shut up, I AM in charge here!" This way of putting it might be a little jarring to us, but it gives a better sense of the invitation, and the challenge contained in the phrase.

So, let us just be still. We take that as the invitation to experience that stillness, and rightly so. But before we can prepare ourselves for that stillness, we may need to listen to that other injunction. Desist! Stop there! Or maybe in Spanish *calmate!* Which means *Stay put and shut up!* Stop all of your hectic running around and looking for God, or for happiness, or for whatever you are looking for, in the wrong places. Stop hankering, clamoring, saying "Where is it? Where is it?" We are enjoined to stop all that, and just be still. Just be. And in that place where all is still, we are able to taste that realm that goes beyond words.

Once again, "Be still, and *Know that I AM God.*" The word "know" may have a connotation of an act of knowing as a subject "knows" an object, but this way of construing it is misleading. The word "confess," as one translation goes, may be helpful to get a better sense of the point at issue here. Know, however, that it is not just confessing, in terms of saying something out loud, "I confess." The meaning here is more like recognizing and acknowledging (that is, acknowledge "God" to be God). What does that acknowledgment entail for our lives? It entails a *metanoia*, a total transformation of our way of looking at things and of our way of being. Just acknowledge *what is,* and do not to try to make it more or less than it is, or different from what it is. Do not fight it, but acknowledge it, and surrender to it. There is a power here beyond what you can grasp, that is in charge, and will let things happen in the way they need to happen, so just sit there and be still, and know that, and be at peace. This way of looking at that phrase, *Be still and know that I am God,* might at least give us a better sense of the richness of the nuance in our particular state of practice.

Thirsting and Yearning for Living Waters

Let us look now, at the second block of phrases, again, for hints as to what this psalm is inviting us to taste and to experience.

In the middle of the world there is a river.
Streams run to it, making glad your cities
Making glad the places where you are known
You flow as the waters of that river
And she shall not be moved
For you are with her
You are the morning that dawns over the quiet waters.

"*In the middle of the world, there is a river. Streams run to it. . . .*"
There is a movie that some of you may have seen, called *A River Runs through It,* directed by Robert Redford, and based on an autobiographical book by Norman Maclean. Without going into the film in detail, it suffices to note here that the "river" that runs through the entire film (and book) represents the stream of living waters that runs through our lives, as the source of our inner nourishment, as the place we can turn to to quench our inner thirst. That river is the ever-bubbling spring that is always in our midst, beckoning us to come and drink. How can we discover that river that runs through all that we have and all that we are? We are dying of thirst, and we so long for that stream.

This cry also reminds us of the lament we find in Psalm 42.

As the hart thrills for the fresh brook,
So do I thrill for you.

We are on a spiritual search because we have acknowledged that thirst in our own lives that can never be satisfied by the pursuit of anything finite. We are on this search for that one important pearl of great price, and we are ready to cast aside anything that stands in our way. We are on the same boat together with all sentient beings, and we all thirst for those running streams, that source of living waters that will quench our thirst.

I am thirsty for you—for my life.
When will I go there?
When will I be seen?
When will I enter your utter presence?

I have swallowed my tears all day and all night
Because people mock me all day, saying
"Where is your beloved? Show us, convince us."

When I remember these things,
My heart pours out within me.
How I journeyed with the pilgrim throngs
My ears alive with thanksgiving songs
Up to your house for the festival—
Why am I downcast and disturbed?

My hope is yet in you.
One day I will thank you
When in you I find wholeness
And my anguish is gone.

How my heart is broken, pours out within me!
Therefore I will remember you
From the land of Jordan, from the peaks of Hermon
From the foothills there.

Deep calls to deep.
In your towering waterfall
Waves and billows drench me.

In the daytime you summon your kindness
And at night you sing to me
A prayer for my life to be living.

So I will rise in the morning and sing to you
My rock, why have you forgotten me?

Why must I walk
Grieving up and down
Oppressed and opposed?
My bones snap.

When the others revile me all day long, saying,
"Where is your beloved? Show me, convince me."
Why is my heart broken, pouring out within me?

My hope is yet in you
And one day I will give you thanks
When I am whole.

If Psalm 42 speaks to us and we can recognize ourselves as the thirsty one crying out for water, then Psalm 46 comes to us as Good News.

In the middle of the world there is a river
Streams run to it, making glad your cities
Making glad the places where you are known

In short, thirst no more: just stop, and drink to your heart's content. Just be still. And you will know. And be filled to the brim.

When we look at ourselves, and acknowledge that thirst within us, we may tend to think that the water we earnestly seek is nowhere to be found, or that we are a long way from finding what we seek. If that is so, we are like the fish in the midst of water asking, where is the water? The fish in its entirety is surrounded by the water, in fact, is already immersed in it, but is not able to see this.

How do we open our eyes to recognize that water that we thirst for and seek so ardently, and let it inundate our lives? How do we satisfy that thirst? Where can we go to drink? The pointer is right there: "*In the middle of the world.*" It is right there, in our very midst, where we can find what we are looking for.

The good news is that what we so earnestly seek is already within reach, right here in our midst. We are invited to open the gates of our own hearts. We remain right in the midst of that for which we are looking, but a barrier within us prevents us from fully recognizing it. It is the barrier of our own resistance to it. For some, that barrier may be thicker than for others, based on the karmic baggage we may have piled up for ourselves. This barrier makes us think that we must still go on striving and struggling for a long time, or that we still have a long way to go.

As we sit in silence, we might just be able to dispose ourselves so that there is some shift of our internal furniture, so that we can acknowledge that barrier in ourselves. Let me first give some descriptions of what we may be undergoing in this light.

The need to quench our inner thirst may have led us to wanting to acquire more possessions, or seeking more power and so on. We may mistakenly believe that those things will satisfy us, not realizing what we really seek is something much deeper than what such surface pursuits can satisfy. We mistakenly believe that in our life in this world we can have power over others, that we can have more control than others who are seen as our rivals. That belief actually aggravates the situation we find ourselves in, compounding the conflict, the opposition, and, subsequently, the violence that already marks our situation in this world. We simply add on to that vicious cycle of opposition and conflict, in joining the bandwagon of seeking more possessions than others, more power than others.

We also may be led to think that we can satisfy our inner thirst by acquiring knowledge through reading. We want to read through all the books we possibly can, even spiritual books, thinking that we will find that for which we seek there. We may find some temporary solace, or may come upon some inspiring insights as we pore over this or that spiritual book we find readily available.

Reading spiritual books can be likened to looking at a recipe or menu, or a book on gourmet cooking. As we read, our appetites are whetted and the juices flow, but if we remain just readers, we will never get to partake of the meal and thus be truly and fully satisfied. Such books serve as guides for us to know how and where to find the food.

Or our inner thirst may drive us to seek all kinds of thrills and pleasures, thinking that these things would satisfy us. We may turn to diversions of the senses, going out for the latest blockbuster films, or following our favorite teams in sports. We may go for the pleasures of the palate, or turn to aesthetic, or other kinds of pursuits that engage us and while away our time. Well and good, as these pursuits are indeed part of "the good life" that we have a right to enjoy and can give us a taste of being alive. But if we look more deeply, we may recognize that we hanker for these things as they take our gaze away from the emptiness we feel within. And so, while these pursuits may afford us some limited kind of satisfaction, after we are through with them, the inner thirst returns, and we go on seeking the next one. And so on, and endlessly so.

As we pause to consider these kinds of hankerings, we may come to recognize that these are symptomatic of a deeper kind of need, a more fundamental kind of want that is at the heart of our human condition.

Our hankering for power and possessions, for knowledge and spiritual insight, for thrills and pleasures can be seen as symptomatic of that deepest longing in our hearts for something infinite, that can be satisfied by nothing less than the realization of the Infinite itself. It is no other than a deep-seated longing in our hearts for infinite being, unrestricted consciousness, unmitigated bliss.

In the Hindu tradition, ultimate reality is called *Brahman*, a term that is derived from the noun form of the verb "to grow, to expand, to increase." In short, that which is called ultimate reality, *Brahman*, is ever growing, ever expanding, beyond what our puny little human minds can capture. This is the implication of the very word "infinite," that is, not finite, not confined to the restrictions that our human minds or human experience can contain. Brahman is always bigger than whatever we can capture with our own human mind, in short, resonating with a medieval European attempt at describing what Christians refer to in using the term "God," it is "that than which nothing greater can be conceived."

In the Hindu tradition this notion of Brahman is associated with the threefold attributes of infinite be-ing (*sat*), all pervading and unrestricted consciousness (*cit*), and unmitigated bliss (*ānanda*). Sages who spent years in deep meditative practice in the forests taught others the way to oneness with Brahman, that is, in recognizing and realizing that what lies at the core of our human hearts, the deepest Self of human beings, called the *Ātman,* is no other than Brahman. In short, in the teaching of the Hindu sages, the way to oneness with the Infinite (Brahman) is through realizing one's own True Self (Ātman), that is, by taking the inward journey to the core of one's own being.

Those three attributes of ultimate reality described above correspond with what we humans yearn for so deeply in our hearts. We are invited to a foretaste of the fullness of being,

all-embracing consciousness, and unmitigated bliss in the stillness of the here and now. Out of this experience of realization
will flow the rivers of living water that can quench our thirst
for a lifetime and enable us to point out to others the way to
the source of this living water.

> *. . . making glad your cities,*
> *making glad the places you are known.*

The NRSV translation of this passage (Ps. 46:4) goes like
this:

> *There is a stream, whose rivulet gladdens the city of God, the*
> *holy dwelling of the Most High.*

This passage invites us experientially to place ourselves
where infinite streams of living water are always flowing that
will enable us to drink our fill—"the city of God [*ir-elohim* in
Hebrew], the holy dwelling of the most high." This resonates
with a term in the Buddhist tradition associated with "the
place of peace." This is *Brahma-vihāra*, which can be translated
as "divine dwelling." Our practice of stillness brings us to this
divine dwelling. It is not something that is waiting for us just
in the next life, but it is accessible right here, right now. In the
silence, we receive the invitation to enter into and to place
ourselves in that divine dwelling, and stay there, and be nour-
ished for a lifetime. We are already there, it is already in our
midst, if we open the eyes of our heart. We are invited to pitch
our tents in that divine dwelling, and know that we are citi-
zens of that divine dwelling.

Let me now outline four characteristics of that divine
dwelling that are developed in Buddhist scriptures. These
are also what are known as the four immeasurables, the four

boundless traits of that divine dwelling. They are called boundless because they cover an infinite range and are unconditioned realities or unconditioned features. The first one is loving-kindness, *mettā*. This is a term in the Pali language, which comes from the Sanskrit term, *maitrī*, which may also be translated as friendship, affinity, kinship. *Mettī* means a deeply felt affinity that generates thoughts of wishing the well-being of one's own kin. And "kin" here embraces all beings.

We have a well-known passage from Buddhist scriptures that speaks of a heart of loving compassion like a mother would have for her only child. The Treatise on Loving-kindness (*Mettā Sutta*) contains this passage: "As a mother would give her life to protect her only child, have this mind (heart) among you toward all beings!" We are to have that heart and mind toward all sentient beings, without exception, without reserve, without exemption, as we are able to regard all sentient beings as our kin. That heart of loving-kindness is a key feature of being in the divine dwelling. We may already recognize that need in ourselves, but perhaps we may remain limited in it. There are certain individuals or certain beings toward whom we naturally feel that loving-kindness. Still, there are others whom we would rather not consider in that same regard because they irritate us or spread gossip about us, or even because they are just out of our horizon or vision. This, however, is the invitation that this divine dwelling is opening to us, to break down those walls that exclude anybody from your range of loving-kindness. All sentient beings are kin to us. We would recognize this kinship if we would just look and see what is.

Kinship is not something that we choose, that is, to regard some as kin, and set aside others. It is a reality we are called to awaken to, as it is the very nature of who we really are, that is, to be kin to one another. One of the very basic expressions of enlightenment that runs through the entire Buddhist tradition is the realization of the interconnectedness of all things in this universe. There is nothing in this universe that stands alone by itself, but each thing, each being exists only insofar as it is related to every other being. As we recognize this kinship with all beings, that heart and mind of loving-kindness cannot but gush forth from where we are. It does not come from our own little charitable wishes, but from the very nature of *what is*. When we have surrendered to what is, the power of what is will overwhelm us and let that natural surge and power of loving-kindness embrace the earth. We are feeble little instruments, called to simply give in to the innate power of loving-kindness opened to us, now directed toward all in an overarching embrace. And the first beneficiaries to that loving-kindness are the ones immediately close to my range of action and relatedness, beginning with my family, my close friends and associates, and on to wider and wider circles of the entire global community with whom we are connected on various levels of our being.

A second characteristic is *karuna*, or compassion, which is the flip side of loving-kindness. When we see fellow beings in a state of suffering or pain, that pain or struggle or suffering is our very own pain, struggle, or suffering. It is not something we observe, as if from the outside and generating pity in us, while thinking, "I'm glad that's not me." Sometimes we can look at another's pain, even if we feel pity, and still we have that mental reservation, "Ah, I'm glad, it is the other and not me." That is not compassion yet. In that though, there is still a lingering notion of the separation between myself and the other. It is only when we bridge that separation, or rather when we overcome that wall of separation, when the other's pain is no longer solely theirs, but my own pain, that we can truly experience this second immeasurable. Compassion is suffering with. Again, we may have already discerned this in ourselves, this natural connectedness with all of creation. For example, we might see a child in pain, and somehow our natural response is to feel for the child, as a free reflective response. This is a manifestation of our true nature. And even with this, we have a second reflection, "Oh, that poor child, I have to help it." There it is again, the "I" that looks at the child as "out there" that I feel "pity" for. We then tend to think, "I want to help this child, whom I pity." With those ideas, we fall back into a dualistic mode of thinking, a separate world of "me" and "them." How, then, can we maintain that prereflective state of oneness in others' pain? And how are we able to live in a social context with distinct individualities but still reach out and embrace others in their pain? This can be a complicated mental task, but if we take it out of our minds and, instead, let this sink into us in the stillness, we may discover something important. We must be able to understand it, not as our mental task to accomplish, but as an invitation to taste and see that *we are the world,* that we are united and intimately interconnected as kin with everyone and everything in the world. Then, we may be able to undergo that *metanoia*, that transformation of our entire minds and hearts, and live from the point of view of the divine dwelling, wherein the separation between the "I" and the world has been overcome.

We may then be able to redirect our own social lives and our own lives in this phenomenal world, grounded in that compassion. That remains a task for each and every one of us, that is, to consider what our own gifts and limitations are, or to live empowered by that compassion and not by pity and not by a sense of wanting to do good for others.

The third element in this divine dwelling is *muditha*, or sympathetic joy. We are able to share the joy of anyone who is also living in joy. Or when there is something to celebrate, we share in that celebration, naturally. We do not complain and covet, thinking, "Oh, I wish it happened to me instead." That, again, is a dualistic thought that blocks the way and prevents us from celebrating. Lurking in our consciousness is the question, "Oh, when do I get my turn?" As long as that thought is still there, then we are still separated from our true selves, and thereby called to break down the wall separating us from others, the wall that blocks us from celebrating in that joy as our very own joy.

And the fourth characteristic of this divine dwelling is called *upekkha*, or equanimity. The word *upekkha* comes from a compound that indicates to see at close hand, to see without any obstructions, to see just as it is, to see everything just as it is. This opens up that immeasurable horizon in us, ushered in by that realization that we are all part of the interconnected wave that enables us to extend loving-kindness to all without exception, to realize that the suffering of all beings is my own suffering, and thus also to be able to share in the joy of each and every being as my own joy. In short, as I am able to live in equanimity, to see things just as they are, the other three aspects of the immeasurable horizon (the divine dwelling) become manifest in my own being and way of life.

The Buddhist scriptures describe these four immeasurables as an ever-bubbling empowerment of living in that place of peace, in that divine dwelling. Those are the four concrete features of living in that divine dwelling, where we have constant access to the living water. Again, this invitation is not only waiting for us in the next life, but it is openly and readily available to us here in this very life, as we undergo that total transformation of mind and heart.

But what are the prescriptions to break down those barriers that prevent us from acknowledging that divine dwelling or having access to it? This is what the guidelines for contemplative practice are all about, which we will address later on. Right now, I just want to offer a scenario of that place where we already are, so in hearing it and in finding that we are already there, it resonates in our being. I want for us to feel a little more at ease and be a little more trusting in our knowledge that we do not need to do anything, and that we can sit and be still and surrender to that reality. How do we surrender?

In letting go of the notion of the self, this "I" that we tend to think is in here somewhere, we open the floodgates of our being that ushers in the divine dwelling. But how do we rid ourselves of the focus on this "I"? A friend recently gave me a book titled *To Shine One Corner of the World: Moments with Shunryu Suzuki* that captures scenes that students of Suzuki remembered. Contained are little anecdotes about events and conversations here and there, which make for delightful reading. Once I opened it, I could not put it down. I would like to share one passage that might provide a hint for us to help us recognize where that flowing stream resides, right in the midst of us. "One day in lectures Suzuki Rōshi said, 'when you are completely absorbed in your breathing, there is no self. What is your breathing? That breathing is not you, nor air. What is it? It is not self at all. When there is no self, you have absolute freedom. Because you have a silly idea of self, you have a lot of problems.'" Suzuki Rōshi has a rather curt way of bidding us to throw away our "silly notions of self." But this is easier said than done.

Let us now just get to that business of breathing. Our breathing provides the key, and we have been breathing all along, since the moment of our births. We need only travel back and become little children again. Everything we are looking for is nowhere else but there where we are already, that is, right here, right now.

Behold in Awe and Wonder

Nations rage, kingdoms tumble—
This is the sound of your voice
This is the earth melting away
You are with us, our defense, our silent center
What we see is all your doing
These desolations
These terrifying moments—
Only our unmoving movement
You cause wars to cease when they cease, to cease forever
You break the bow, snap the spear
Burn up the war wagons.

Looking back at the ground covered so far, we have considered where we can find our refuge. We have also noted that as we go deeper into this practice of stillness, fear can begin to creep in on us. To work through this fear, we need simply to look at it straight in the eye, and not recoil from it nor be dissuaded from continuing in our practice. As we see through these fears and go beyond them, as we continue in this contemplative practice, we may arrive at the place where we are able to take a sip from those living waters that flow deep within. *You are with us, our defense, our silent center.*

To find this place of refuge, and to dwell in it, is to dwell in "the city of God," the "divine dwelling," and from there, generate the four immeasurables: loving-kindness for all creation, a deep and genuine compassion with the openheartedness that bears the suffering of all, the ability to share the joy of all those celebrating, and a deep sense of equanimity, calm, and tranquility, grounded in the ability to see things as they truly are.

Firmly grounded in that divine dwelling, we are able to exclaim, in awe and wonder: *What we see is all your doing.*

The NRSV translates this as "*Come; behold the deeds of the LORD.*"

This remains a standing invitation, and it is being offered to us in every moment. "Come and behold!" In other words, Come and see for yourselves, all these wonderful things being described here in words!

We recall a scene in the New Testament that resonates with this passage. Two disciples ask Jesus, "Where is your dwelling?" And Jesus responds with an invitation to them: "Come and see." This is an invitation for us also.

Turning to Buddhist tradition, when people encountered Shakyamuni, the Awakened One, they were amazed and immediately drawn to him. They sought to learn from him so they might become like him, imbued with deep inner peace, with the wisdom of seeing things as they are, and with a heart of compassion for all beings. They asked him to teach them the way to arrive at that place of peace that he had realized, so they too might become like him. Rather than giving them doctrines or teachings or telling them what to believe or think, his most immediate response was this: *ehi passiko,* in Pali, which means, "Come and see."

Come and see. If we study the earlier strata of Buddhist scriptures, those that reflect the exchanges between the Awakened One and his disciples, we find that when the disciples would query him about something, rather than giving them a doctrinal answer, he would respond with a set of practical guidelines for discovering the answer for themselves.

One such example is the story of the woman who had suffered the death of her toddler whom she loved dearly. The child's death distressed her so much that she would not even take the step to bury him. Even a couple of days after the child's death, she still clung to him, thinking "I want my child back. I want my child back." Having heard of the reputation of this Buddha, who was supposed to be all-wise and all compassionate, she went to him, asking him, "Please give me back my child." The Buddha's response was said to be the following: "I will do so on condition that you go and bring back a grain of mustard seed." And the woman thought, hmm, well that is easy enough. "But it must be a grain of mustard seed from a house where nobody has died." So the woman, thinking this would ease her grieving, goes to one house and asks for a mustard seed, but first asks, "Has anybody died in this house?" The first homeowner she approaches tells her that his grandfather died just three weeks ago. Hearing this, she knows she cannot accept the mustard seed. So she goes from house to house until she has exhausted herself having visited every house in the village, without finding a single house wherein death had not occurred. In the process of all those conversations and all that visiting, somehow she comes to a realization that death is an unavoidable fact of life. This realization as such cannot be conveyed adequately in descriptive sentences, being a transformative experience. But we only need imagine the process she underwent as she doggedly knocked on every door of every house hoping to find one where no death had occurred. In so doing, she eventually came to the realization that death is everywhere, that it is unavoidable, that it is part of life itself, and, more important, that it is not something to be feared.

With this realization, she is able to see her own dead son with eyes of equanimity, and quietly does what she needs to do in this regard, that is, bury him and give him due honors for a memorial, still mourning him but now no longer clinging to him, and now able to feel gratitude for the short span of life he was granted to be with her, his mother. And with that, she is freed from her attachment, and subsequently she becomes a follower of the Buddha, or so the story goes. In short, the Buddha's way of responding to those who ask for guidance on the path to enlightenment is simply, "Come and see for yourself."

How do we take this invitation? Where do we go from here? We tell the Buddha, "You told us to 'come and see,' so here we are. Where, and what now?"

In response, we find handed down to us the centuries-old traditions of meditative practice in the Buddhist tradition. If we are to regard those as concrete guidelines to "come and see" as the Buddha beckons us, we may note the common strand throughout these traditions, which is the affirmation that we do not have to go anywhere but we need only be right here, right now. Stay where you are, and open your eyes. Let us just take these two points, *stay where you are*, and *open your eyes*.

Let us see what we might be able to glean from these that might occasion the opening of our own eyes, as we take the cue from those who have followed the invitation before us.

In the New Testament, we note a passage where Jesus says, "Whoever sees me, sees the Father." The verb "to see" in Greek is *theorein*, from which we get the English word "theory." The meaning of the Greek, however, is not "theory" in the English sense, but rather "to behold, to look at," in a mode of direct seeing. In the fourth gospel, this verb *theorein* and another verb, *pisteuein*, "to believe, to trust," are very closely linked. The point of this verb is not that we believe "that something is the case," but that we believe in and entrust our whole being to that reality, and in doing so, we are enabled to see that reality as it is. Especially in the fourth gospel, the ideas of *pisteuein* and *theorein* blend together. In the Christian tradition the notions believing and seeing remain interlinked.

There is an ancient Hebrew tradition that held that no one may see the Divine Glory and remain alive. "You cannot see

My face, for no one may see me and live" (Exod. 33:20). That is why Moses was only allowed to see the "back side" of God in his experience of the burning bush. If one happens to get a glimpse of the glory of God, the *kavod adonai*, it is said that then one melts away, because of the intensity of that experience, and dies.

A passage from Shunryu Suzuki's well-known and widely read book, *Zen Mind, Beginner's Mind*, may also offer us a hint here. It echoes the one cited earlier from the collection of his sayings, *To Shine One Corner of the World:* "When you are breathing, and truly breathing, there is no room for that little self to jut into place. When you are breathing, just breathe, and when you are standing, just stand. And when you are eating, just eat. And when you are truly there, where is that little self, where is the self there? When you are truly there, then that is precisely an indication that that little self, that self-conscious mind has died, and is fully given over to what is." Let us take that as a hint.

In the Zen tradition, central place is given to what is known as the enlightenment experience, the awakening experience called *kensho*, a compound in Japanese which means "to see one's true nature." What is this "true nature" that is to be seen? We all seek the True Self, or, in our Christian terms, we yearn to behold the face of God, and thereby taste eternal life. Such seeing, in poetic words, give us "intimations of immortality," those glimpses that take us beyond the realm accessible to our five senses. So *kensho* is that event whereby one sees one's true nature, and in being able to do so, in Zen tradition, one thus becomes an Awakened One, that is, a Buddha.

To see one's true nature, that which one truly is, is to become a Buddha, to become awakened. This is to die to our little self, to die to that self-conscious mind that is always watching over things from a separated place, seeking to get in control, tending to make judgments and comparisons. Some may come to it in a sudden moment, an unexpected "aha!" moment that transforms one's outlook on things definitively from that point on. Some may just experience it in a quiet way, without any fanfare or emotional outburst, except for that quiet joy that ensues. Such persons simply move along this path of awakening in a process of gradual transformation, and are able to live in that world of enlightenment without all of the paraphernalia attached to it that one reads about in popular Zen literature. There are those among us who live in that life of wisdom and compassion but who do not need to put it on their shoulders or on their lapels. And we know that this is genuine, when it does not have to be ostentatiously displayed to others, as if to say, "Hey, look, everybody, I'm enlightened!"

The Zen tradition offers us a methodical way in which individuals can come to this practice of seeing their True Self and thus being free of their ego-delusions. There are two basic approaches by which one can pursue this path. The first is the way of "just sitting," referred to as *shikantaza* in Japanese. This way is mostly prescribed in the Soto tradition, where at every moment of our daily, waking life from early in the morning to late at night, we are invited simply just to be there, standing up, just standing up, sitting down, just sitting down, just being there, moment after moment after moment, fresh and new each time. During sitting, it is just sitting, breathing in and breathing out. The instruction toward this mode of sitting begins with instructions on how to count the breath so that the mind comes to focus on each breath, allowing it to be present in each here and now, not letting it get lost in meanderings all over the place.

Suzuki Rōshi, cited earlier, invites each of us to come back always to the beginner's state of mind, with that freshness that enables us to welcome and appreciate each moment of our day-to-day life just as it is, for what it is. "Beginner's mind" may sound rather simple, but as one engages in actual Zen practice, one realizes that it is far from being "easy." This expression "beginner's mind" is in fact another way of describing an enlightened mind.

Another tradition is the Rinzai (Linji in Chinese) Zen, a lineage that makes use of devices called *koans*. Koans can be helpful in cracking the self-conscious mind with which one always tries to figure things out and which wants to be in control and see the rational side of everything. It places before that rational mind a conundrum or an unsolvable puzzle, unsolvable, that is, within the parameters and limits of that rational mind.

As one just breathes in and breathes out with a mind focused on the breathing, not even being aware and conscious of the breath, but just breathing in and breathing out, being fully there, and then some sound emerges, like a whistle, or a bark of a dog, or a sneeze of someone in the room—in that state of openness and transparency, such a sound may trigger an opening to a new realm that "no eye has seen nor ear heard." In such a moment, one can come to an awakening, whereby one realizes that there is *no one there* hearing, and there is nothing to be heard: this is a moment of *just that*. Such a moment can be a revelation of mystery and enable one to see through the koan, "*Who hears?*"

Practice with a koan leads one to a deepening into that stillness that is the fountain of all the discoveries—seeing through the mystery of who we are, what this universe is about. The koan helps in blocking the path of the discursive mind that always wants to figure things out, objectify them, separate them, capture them, and put them into little boxes or categories made up by our own little mind.

There is no way to solve a koan by the conventional methods of rational intellect. It is when the discursive intellect that desires to know and be in control surrenders that we may be enabled to receive the gift of awakening, that is, seeing through the reality of *what is, just as it is.*

A passage from Paul's first letter to the Corinthians echoes this, when it describes that realm "where no eye has seen, nor ears heard" (1 Cor. 2:9).

Searching for True Self

Practice with the koan *mu* can be a powerful way of arriving at this experience of "seeing" what "no eye has seen." The koan goes,

> *A monk asks Joshu in all earnestness, does a dog have Buddha nature or not?*

> *Joshu answered, Mu.*

The practitioner's task is to take this answer of Joshu and let it be one's guide to entering that stillness. *Mu* is not a word with a meaning, but a simple one-syllabic sound; it is like a big opaque block that gives the mind no room to speculate about it. It can stop the usual ways the mind tries to figure something out. The mind is faced with a blank wall, and one is enjoined to just continue breathing in and breathing out, focusing one's entire mind and entire being on this silent sound *muuuu.* One can practice with this for months or years and years, and some have done so before making any headway.

Let me just read to you a passage from someone who was on the Way, on the path toward awakening, having been given this koan *Mu.*

This is from *The Three Pillars of Zen* compiled and edited by Philip Kapleau, an American student of my teacher's teacher (Yasutani Hakuun Rōshi), who studied in the Sanbo Zen tradition and then came back to the United States and taught that tradition to others.

The trouble is, I can't forget myself. I am always aware of myself as subject confronting mu as object. It sounds familiar does it not? I focus my mind on mu, and when I can hang on to it, I think, good, now you've got it. Don't let go. Then I tell myself, no you mustn't think good; you must think only mu. So I clench my hands and bear down with every muscle and eventually something clicks. I know I've reached a deeper level of consciousness, because no longer am I aware of inside or out, front or back. Exhilarated, I think, now I am getting close to enlightenment. Every thought vanished, enlightenment will hit me at any moment. But then I realize I can't be close to enlightenment so long as I am thinking of enlightenment, so my hold on mu loosens and mu is gone again.[2]

This is a familiar story, just running around in circles. But how does this person get around that? It is a long passage, so if you want to read it at some point, it is the one that says, P K, age 46, an American ex-businessman. From this account, we can tell how his search for awakening came from a very sincere and earnest heart. He notes in his account, "Now I know why I tired so quickly of church and synagogue services in the United States. The priests and rabbis and ministers obviously had no intimate experience of a God they preached so glibly about. That is why their sermons and ceremonies were stale and lifeless."[3]

---

[2] Philip Kapleau, ed., *The Three Pillars of Zen*, Revised and Expanded (New York: Anchor Books, 1980), 31.

[3] Ibid., 233.

Again a ring of recognition comes for some of us, perhaps. As he continues his account, we find out that this person, in the course of his own search and earnest Zen practice, arrived at an experience opening him into that world of Zen. This kind of experience can also come to us in ways or in times we least expect. There are degrees of intensity and degrees of depth and of breadth, but even one little such opening can enable us to see that there is much more than meets the eye in this world in which we are plunged to live our lives on this earth.

I would like to share with you another passage of another seeker who came to Japan all the way from Germany in the 1930s to learn Zen and the martial arts. Eugen Herrigel wrote a book called *Zen and the Art of Archery*, which describes his inner journey into the heart of Zen. He began with trying to learn the art of archery, and he was always told, you are not doing it right because you're not breathing right. Here is the passage about that breathing process as he describes it.

I cannot think back to those days without recalling over and over again how difficult I found it in the beginning to get my breathing to work out right. Though I breathed in, technically the right way, whenever I tried to keep my arm and shoulder muscles relaxed while drawing the bow, the muscles of my legs stiffened all the more violently, as though my life depended on a firm foothold, and a secure stance and as though like Antious, I had to draw strength from the ground. Often the master had no alternative but to pounce quickly as lightning on one of my leg muscles and press it in a particularly sensitive spot. When, to excuse myself, I once remarked that I was conscientiously making an effort to keep relaxed, he replied, that is just the trouble. You make an effort to think about it. Concentrate entirely on your breathing as if you had nothing else to do. It took me considerable time before I succeeded in what the master

*wanted, but I succeeded. I learned to lose myself so effort-
lessly in the breathing, that I sometimes had the feeling that
I, myself, was not breathing, but strange as this may sound,
being breathed. Even when, in hours of thoughtful reflection
I struggled against this idea, I could no longer doubt that the
breathing held out all that the master had promised. Now and
then, and in the course of time, more and more frequently, I
managed to draw the bow and keep it drawn until the moment
of release while remaining completely relaxed in body, without
being able to say how it happened. The qualitative difference
between these few successful shots and the innumerable failures
was so convincing that I was ready to admit that now, at last,
I understood what was meant by drawing the bow spiritually.
That was it: not a technical trick I had tried in vain to pick up,
but liberating breath—control with new and far-reaching possibilities. I just want to note that that word control may be misleading. It is not so much controlling the breath but a liberating
way of breathing with new and far-reaching possibilities. I say
this, not without misgivings, for I well know how great is the
temptation to succumb to a powerful influence and ensnared
in self-delusion to over-rate the power of an experience merely
because it is so unusual, but despite all equivocation and civil
reserve, the results obtained by this new breathing were far
too definite to be denied. In talking it over with Mr. Koma-
chia, I once asked him why the master had looked on so long
at my futile efforts to draw the bow spiritually, why he had
not insisted upon the correct breathing from the start. A great
master, he replied, must also be a great teacher. With us, the
two things go hand in hand. Had he begun the lessons with
breathing exercises, he would never have been able to convince
you that you owe them any thing decisive. You had to suffer
a shipwreck through your own efforts before you were ready
to seize the life-belt he threw you. Believe me; I know from*

my own experience that the master knows you and each of his
pupils better than we know ourselves. He reads in the souls of
his pupils more than they care to admit.[4]

This is a story of a person trying to learn the art of archery and also of Zen. The point I wanted to raise with it is that he notes how if he had been taught breathing exercises right from the start, then it would have become just another technique, and he would have had more difficulty. But now, he gets the sense that somehow the key to learning the art of archery that he so wanted to master was in the breathing. He now realizes that if he just went on doing movements in archery as he thought he should, he would fail entirely, so he was open to starting all over again, with learning how to breathe. That was the point when he was ready to learn.

When we are shipwrecked, when we realize we cannot do it by our own small-minded though determined efforts, we need to set everything aside and begin with a totally open heart and mind. That becomes the turning point in our practice. That is the point when we give up our own efforts and our own ideas, and say, "I do not know how to go about it. I have lost the way. Please show me." We need to learn from those times in our own lives when we were totally lost and left without any strength of our own. It is only then that the work of grace can really have room to enter and embrace us. Zen Buddhism may not use this term "grace" which comes from the Christian tradition, but as one experiences those moments of total helplessness and powerlessness, wherein something truly significant and transformative can and does happen, this is the word that most aptly comes to mind for me.

---

[4] Eugen Herrigel, *Zen and the Art of Archery* (New York: Vintage Books, 1981), 23.

I would like to note a couple of other points from an author I read in my own early formation. After coming to Japan and really reading and knowing and learning how to read Japanese, one of the first books I read in Japanese is a book later translated into English by Keiji Nishitani, with the English title, *Religion and Nothingness*. The original Japanese title, *Shūkyō to wa Nanika*, in direct translation, is simply, *What Is Religion?* Nishitani is a philosopher of the Kyoto School who is also very much influenced by the Zen tradition, like many of his colleagues in that school. One of the questions that jumped out at me in my own practice when I read this book was, "What is that which is neither being nor non-being?" The central theme of the whole book is what he calls *absolute nothingness*, which he distinguishes from "relative nothingness," that is, the idea of "nothing" that is opposed to the idea of "something." "Absolute nothingness" is that which transcends that distinction between "something that is" and "something that is not."

On analysis, we can see how our commonsense world is based on the interactions between our subjective consciousness and things out there that we perceive as objects of this subjective consciousness. There are birds out there making chirping sounds, and there is the hearer in here listening to those sounds. After a while, the chirping is no longer heard, and so our mind may go into a discursive process, thinking, "There was a sound before, and now there is no sound." Or, "There was a bird out there, and now there is no bird." In short, "there is" and "there is not" are concepts that are put in dualistic opposition to each other. "To be" or "not to be"— that is the question that the mind keeps pondering, and we are deluded that it has to be one or the other.

The whole world of computers is based on that binary opposition between one and zero, corresponding to the binary opposition of "exists" or "does not exist." For Nishitani, grounded on his own Zen experience, he is inviting us to see the world that is neither zero nor one. This is the realm beyond the opposition of being and nonbeing, or existing and not existing. What is that? This is the theme that he expounds on in his book *Religion and Nothingness*. That is what we are invited to experience.

In realizing that world which totally goes beyond our ordinary mind-set and which we are talking about here, it does not mean that we disappear; we simply go beyond that dualistic opposition between "I am" and "I am not." When you say, "I am," the tendency is to think that there is this "I" who is here, and there are others out there, and so I am not nothing and they are not nothing. Incidentally, Martin Heidegger published a book in his later years titled *Introduction to Metaphysics*, in which he begins with the question, "Why are there existents [beings], rather than nothing?" Insofar as we ask the question in that light, something is here and not the other way around—it is not nothing—then we are still dealing with those oppositional notions. But the key point here is, what is that that is even beyond nothing and something, which is neither existent nor nonexistent? That is the question that confronts the reader of Nishitani's book.

Let me summarize, taking another point that Nishitani offers, which may help us on our own paths to awakening. In one verse he describes what he calls the "standpoint of emptiness," the standpoint where you are able to go beyond the dualistic opposition between something and nothing.

From the pine tree, learn of the pine tree. From the bamboo, learn of the bamboo.[5]

This is not saying, "I am looking at the bamboo, or pine tree, and I analyze its color or its hue, trying to determine its

---

[5] Keiji Nishitani, *Religion and Nothingness*, trans. Jan van Bragt (Berkeley: University of California Press, 1982), 128.

scientific properties." That is the dualistic world—"I" (subject, ego-consciousness) am looking at the "bamboo" (object, that which my ego grasps as "out there" before it, separate from it). When we just come back to that stillness and let that self-conscious judgmental and rationalistic "I" recede into the background, something might emerge from that stillness. In that stillness, the bamboo is simply *right there.* We are invited to "learn from the bamboo." This can happen only when there is no longer an "I" looking at the bamboo as an object out there. I find no way of describing this adequately, except to invite each one to just listen to your own experiences and search through your own experiences and your own history for similar experiences. You may have glimpsed something wherein literally the veil that covers our eyes from seeing has been lifted, even momentarily, and we see that something is really much more than meets the eye, when we see beyond that opposition between something and nothing, and then we truly *see.*

Those are moments that indicate for us that all this is grace, pure grace. I am at a loss of words to describe it, except to repeat what the Psalm has already offered for us. "*Come and behold; Be still and know.*" And you will see "what no eye has seen," and you will hear "what no ear has heard." Let us return to that stillness. The invitation is to let this stillness be part of our lives. Let this stillness be the place we can always come back and find everything we have ever been looking for and everything we need in this life to enable us to become God's gift to the world, as we have found God's gift to us. The infinite loving presence enables us to realize also each and every one of us is a gift to each other. Let us keep coming back to that stillness as our home. As we dwell in that place of stillness, we experience inner peace, and deep, deep gratitude wells up from within. We know we are in good hands, no matter what, for the rest of our days.

Chapter Two

Drawn by an Inner Thirst title follows.

My Cup Overflows (Psalm 23)

Drawn by an Inner Thirst

When anyone comes to our Zen center seeking guidance in this practice, they are asked, What do you seek in taking on this practice? What are you looking for? What led you to come here to learn about Zen?

There are usually four kinds of responses. The first is by those who happen to have been drawn by curiosity, wishing to check out what this whole business of Zen is all about. Or some come through an urging by a friend or family member that they could not decline, who might have told them that Zen might "do them good." A second kind of response comes from those who are drawn to Zen practice because of the health benefits it promises to those who practice it. Indeed, there has been much research on the beneficial effects of meditation on physical and spiritual health in general. It is known to lower blood pressure, increase metabolism, or help in the healing of certain forms of physical ailments, most notably cancer. Meditation is also known to reduce stress, and thereby it leads to a more wholesome lifestyle. A third kind of response comes from those who are ready to engage in Zen practice as they seek inner peace in their hectic lives. Others seek healing of an inner wound, or a resolution of some personal conflict that throws them off balance in their lives. A fourth kind of response is from those who seek meaning in their lives, having come to a direct experience of human mortality through the death of a friend or loved one, or through a medical diagnosis of a possible terminal illness. Or it could be a sense of ennui, an acute sense of the lack of direction in one's life that leads them to ask the big questions, "What is the point of all this?" "Who am I, really?"

For those who begin Zen out of curiosity, having received the initial guidelines and having tried it out to some extent, they may say, "Okay, now I know what it's about, but it's not for me," and go on to something else. Some, after trying it for a little while, may find that meditation practice resonates with something deep in themselves, so they now go into it with a renewed motivation and resolve, and continue the practice on a new level of appreciation and personalized commitment. Those who seek physical benefits may be able to get what they are seeking to some extent, and continue insofar as they are able to reap those benefits but stop if they feel they have attained what they sought in having taken it on in the first place. Or they may also find the practice resonating with them at a deeper level and thus engage it with renewed commitment.

Our orientation sessions offer practical guidelines that can launch anyone willing to engage in it into a deeper level of awareness, a more enhanced appreciation of one's own life.

This deeper level of awareness and enhanced appreciation of one's life can come with a realization that human life lived mainly in the pursuit of gratification of desires tends to leave one eventually unsatisfied and longing for "something more."

Is that all there is?—as the well-known song of Peggy Lee so eloquently put it, we notice an underlying thirst deep in the core of our being, a thirst that cannot be quenched by the pursuit of pleasures, power, or possessions. What Zen offers then, is a set of pointers whereby one might quench this inner thirst, with practical instructions on "how to drink." These instructions involve taking a proper posture conducive to stillness, breathing with attention, and calming the mind by allowing it to rest in the present moment.

There are specific guidelines for posture during seated meditation, as well as guidelines for how we may walk, how we may take our meals, how we recline or go to take our rest, and so on, in ways that are conducive to stillness and mindfulness. During our twenty-four-hour day we can hold ourselves in a way that is conducive to inner stillness, to a mindful way of life, whether it be while standing, in various forms of activity, or reclining.

Once the instructions for taking a posture conducive to stillness in its various modes are set in place, the guidelines proceed to the second point, that is, paying attention to the breath. One is to breathe in the most natural way, with awareness of each breath as one inhales, and then exhales, and then inhales again, and so on. We are invited to come to a distinctive awareness of this mysterious event that happens every moment of our lives but which we tend to take for granted. We tend to think that breathing is simply a biophysical phenomenon that happens all the time, and not be able to recognize its vital importance in our lives.

Truly, the breath is the master key to unravel the very mystery of our lives. Consider this: breathing is really at the center of what is happening in our lives from day to day, from moment to moment. One could say that our entire life consists mainly in just breathing in, and breathing out. The moment we are born we start breathing, with a big "uhaaa" that we utter as we come out of our mother's womb. The moment we die, we stop breathing. Or conversely, when we stop breathing, we die. That's it. Saying it this way makes it seem rather obvious, but this tells us of the intimate connection between the breath and our very life.

The third point in the set of guidelines for Zen practice, intimately linked to the second that relates to breathing, consists in bringing the mind to rest in the present moment, to a point of stillness. We are instructed to allow our mind to be right here, right now, and not be looking for or thinking about something else, or imagining something in the past or in the future. We are to place the mind just where our breathing is, so that it is right here, right now, with every breath. We direct our minds such that they are attentive to the here and now, with every breath. When we are walking, we cultivate a mind that is attentive to every moment as we step, and as we take the next step, and the next, and so on.

These then are the three elements to put in place in Zen practice: appropriate posture, breathing with awareness, and a mind disposed to stillness. As we sit, walk, take our meals, or do our chores, the mind is also invited to just be there, where we are, and not let it go all over the place thinking of other things, but to just be attentive in whatever situation we may be in. Being attentive, in short, is our way of preparing ourselves to drink and thus quench our inner thirst: it disposes our heart and mind to open up to the infinite realm waiting in every moment.

Calling on the Unnamable

Psalm 23 will be our starting point for going into the depths of the Zen experience that may enable our hearts to drink and be quenched of its thirst. Let us first look at the translation of this Psalm by Zen Master Norman Fischer.

You are my Shepherd. I am content.
You lead me to rest in the sweet grasses to lie down by the quiet waters
And I am refreshed.
You lead me down the right path, the path that
    unwinds in the pattern of your name.
And even if I walk through the valley of the
    shadow of death, I will not fear,
For you are with me
Comforting me with your rod and your staff, showing me each step.
You prepare a table for me in the midst of my adversity
And moisten my head with oil
Surely my cup is overflowing
And goodness and kindness will follow me all the days of my life
And in the long days beyond I will always live within your house.

This is a well-known psalm known by many under the title "The Lord Is My Shepherd."

The first word, replaced by "You" in our Zen translation, is "The Lord" in the English translations most of us are familiar with. In the Hebrew, this is written as four letters (a "tetragram"), YHWH. These four letters seek to convey the name of the Holy One that Moses encountered when he was before the burning bush at Mount Sinai. Some scholars or biblical translators render that as "Yahweh," but for those within the Jewish tradition, to say this name out loud is somewhat close to a blasphemy, something that may be taken as offensive by the devout in this religious community.

Let me give an example. The Japanese people have a particular sentiment toward the emperor of Japan that dates back to the seventh century of our common era. They feel that the emperor is the protector, the father, the one who really is the center of their being as a people, and they regard him with a very distinctive kind of reverence. They never refer to the emperor by his first name. Non-Japanese often say "Hirohito" (the Japanese emperor during the Second World War and several decades of the postwar years), or "Akihito" (the current emperor). For Japanese ears, to hear a non-Japanese person say "Hirohito" or "Akihito" in referring to their emperor is somewhat jarring, as it is a name that they revere and would never say out loud themselves. It points to a realm that touches the center of their being, the realm of the sacred for them. So they go around this and refer to the emperor as "His Imperial Highness" or "His Imperial Majesty" (*Tennō Heika*), using the third person, and in a highly reverential manner at that. That is just an analogy of the cultural context wherein the name of the Holy One is not pronounced out loud.

For the Israelites, for the Hebrews, for religious Jews, that term YHWH is so sacred, even writing it like that is something done with fear and trembling. The religious Jews and the people who took this as their tradition would move around the sacredness by calling it *Adonai*, the Lord, or the Master, the Boss, or "the Holy Name" (*Ha Shem*), referring to it obliquely in the third person.

For Moses it came as revelation of the Holy One in their midst, whom he encountered at the burning bush on Mount Sinai, and the Holy One assured him, "I have seen the suffering of my people . . . so I have come down to liberate them . . . and I will be with you" (Exod. 3:7, 8, 12). He hears the command to go to the pharaoh of Egypt to ask for freedom for his people. Moses then asks, "Who shall I say has sent me? What is his name?" The words that came in response are rendered in Roman letters as *ehyeh asher ehyeh*. This comes from the Hebrew verb *hawah* (הוה), which can be translated as "to be." This verb is also related to the literal meaning of the tetragram YHWH.

Moses asks, "Who is it that is sending me?" The answer he gets is *Ehyeh asher ehyeh*. Another approximate rendering of this in English is "I will be as I will be," since in Hebrew grammar, the present is open to the future. This was rendered by Thomas Aquinas in Latin as *ego sum qui sum*, *"I am who am,"* as a more common rendering in English. In shorter form, simply, I AM.

Sitting in stillness prepares us for an encounter of the kind that Moses experienced at the burning bush. We are drawn to this practice of sitting in stillness by our own big question in our lives: Who am I? And who is it that is sending me forth, breath by breath, into this life?

Who are you? Well, when we are asked this question, we tend to answer with an identifying label, "I am so and so (given name)." Or, we may answer by saying what we "do" on a continual basis. "I am a doctor." "I am a student." "I am a lawyer." "I am cook." "I am a housewife." "I am a minister." Or we may respond to the question by naming a particular relationship that the questioner may understand. "I am the son or daughter of so and so." We usually tag on a very concrete form to that "I am. . . ," which thereby marks our identity in distinction from other identities. Those tags determine our form in this world. I am this, I am that, thus delimiting it in a very concrete way. We, of course, live in this world that is finite, and we need to determine that concrete form that makes us "who we are." But if we think that is all we are, then we are missing the point. We are only looking at the form, like the tip of the iceberg of who we are. That which you can describe in words or in concepts or by what you do or what you have really is just like this tip of the iceberg.

There is a group psychological exercise in which the participants are paired; taking turns, one partner asks the other repeatedly, "Who are you?" At first the respondent usually answers by giving his or her name. But the questioner keeps repeating, "Who are you?" The respondent may then answer, "I am the son or daughter of so and so." But again, the question is asked. "Who are you?" The responses then continue, "I bake bread." "I take care of children." "I drive a cab." And so on. And again, and again, the question is repeated. Who are you? The responses may go to other facets of one's life as one perceives it, describing one's temperament, likes and dislikes, tendencies, and so on. "I am a thoughtful person." "I am musically inclined." "I am tone-deaf." Continuing that pattern for ten or fifteen minutes, inevitably the person being asked will run out of things to say that have not already been said, in response to the question, "Who are you?" There is a lull of silence. That is the point when something important might come up as new revelation to that person. "You are all that, yes, but that is not all you are." That lull of silence can be an "aha" moment that allows one a glimpse of the depths that lie beneath one's own consciousness, toward which the question "Who am I?" points.

Who are you? As we peel off those things that we associate with our identity one by one, we are enabled to see that "Who I am" is not just those things that can be named and described in answer to the question, but that there is something deeper in us that simply cannot be captured in words. In that moment of silence as one's mind is stopped in its tracks by the inability to give any further answers to the question, there might just be something that will open up and enable us to realize that what we truly are is something that can never be described in words. We may have been living as if those labels or descriptions about who we are that came out in words define who we are, but now we may be able to realize that there is "something more." So, in seeing that what can be put in words is only a tip of the iceberg of who and what we are, we might be able to touch that place where it leads to the depths of the iceberg, and we may be able to glimpse something that opens us to a realm beyond words, a realm that is truly infinite.

I invite us all to take that as our hint for plunging into the depths of that reality that we are that is timeless, that is boundless, but at the same time that which connects us with each and every concrete form visible and manifest in this universe, on this earth where we are living together. For this, the practical guideline I offer here is to simply sit, breathing in and breathing out, and accompanying the outbreath with the sound of "I AM." For now, I would like to invite everyone to sit still, breathing in and breathing out, and immerse yourself in that sound, I AM.

With the out-breath, listen to that. I AM. Let that resonate, and let yourself dissolve in that. I AM. Do not let that just be tacked on to particular things. There is no particular thing that limits it, but precisely in uttering I AM, when you look at that tree outside, you will realize, it is included in that I AM. When you touch the earth and you hear the rustle of leaves as you walk on the dried leaves, it is that I AM. When you look at the stars at night and see the twinkle, it is that I AM.

Let us listen from the depths to that dimension of our being. We are not dealing here with a concept that we can capture with our thinking mind. As we sit in stillness, let us set aside all those concepts and just taste each moment, breathing in and breathing out, taking this step, taking that step, hearing the bell, ggooonnnnnnggg, going back to the main hall, taking our meal, taking our rest. In each moment of our day, let us just bask ourselves in this I AM, and taste and see. I AM.

Let us take Psalm 23 as our guide on our journey within, our return home. The entire psalm provides a horizon for us and invites each of us to let it resonate in our own being, especially in the context of sitting in silence and letting us just come home to every breath. For those who have taken the suggestion to just breathe in and breathe out, resonate with *I am*. Listen to the psalm resonating with that revelation of *I am*, hearing it from within our own very being, that *I am* that we are all also enveloped by and that we identify with as we breathe in and breathe out.

> *I AM is my shepherd, I shall not want.*
> *In burdened pastures, I AM gives me repose.*
> *Beside restful waters, I AM leads me.*
> *I AM refreshes my soul.*
> *I AM guides me in the right paths for the sake of the name of I AM.*
> *Even though I walk in the dark valley, I fear*
> *   no evil, for you are with me.*
> *With your rod and your staff, you give me courage.*
> *You spread the table before me in the sight of my oppressors.*
> *You anoint my head with oil.*
> *My cup overflows.*
> *Only goodness and kindness follow me all the days of my life.*
> *And I shall dwell in the house of I AM for years and years to come.*

Now I would like to just come back to that key phrase, the key expression that jumps at us from this psalm. *I AM is my shepherd.* This was, as I noted, presented to Moses when he was confronted by that burning bush and he began to wonder what sort of thing this was. Then he heard the message. Here is the passage where that encounter happens in the book of Exodus, chapter 3:

> *When I AM saw Moses coming over to look at the bush more closely, he called out to him from the bush, "Moses." Moses answered, "Here I am." Then I AM said, "Come*

no nearer. Remove the sandals from your feet, for the place where you stand is holy ground. I am the God of your father," he continued. "The God of Abraham, the God of Isaac, the God of Jacob." Moses hid his face because he was afraid to look at God, but I AM said, "I have witnessed the affliction of my people in Egypt and I have heard their cry of lament against their slave drivers. I know well what they are suffering. Therefore, I have come down to rescue them from the hands of their oppressors and lead them out of that land into a good and spacious land, a land flowing with milk and honey."

The first point I would like to offer for our own tasting, as we breathe in and breathe out, and enable that expression to sink in, is this I AM. Let us open our ears to the dimensions of that I AM. I AM that sees the afflictions of all people, the I AM that feels the pain of all those in suffering in this world. Let us see, hear, taste, touch, and feel that suffering of the earth with those eyes of I AM. That is one point I would like to offer. And you may just dwell on that. It may take you quite a long time to sit with that, perhaps the whole rest of your life, in fact. That I AM embraces all the pains of the world, all the wounds of the earth, all the sufferings of the people, and of all sentient beings. Let us just let that resonate within, and then out of that pain, out of that sharing of that suffering, will come forth whatever we are called to offer. I will come down and rescue my people from their suffering. It is that same I AM hearing that suffering, hearing that crying, that will come forth and offer whatever can be offered for its healing.

This passage reminds me so much of a poem written by Thich Nhat Hanh, which is known to many if not most of us, which also resonates with repeated affirmations of I AM. This poem is titled "Please Call Me by My True Names." I would

like to provide that for you also, to help in understanding this
I AM in its implications and in its dimensions. Thich Nhat
Hanh writes in his book *Being Peace:*

> *Do not say that I'll depart tomorrow—*
> *Because even today I still arrive.*
> *Look deeply. I arrive in every second*
> *To be a bud on a spring branch,*
> *To be a tiny bird with wings still fragile,*
> *Learning to sing in my new nest,*
> *To be a caterpillar in the heart of flower,*
> *To be a jewel hiding in itself in a stone.*
> *I still arrive in order to laugh,*
> *To cry, in order to fear and hope*
> *The rhythm of my heart is the birth and death of all that are alive.*
> *I am the mayfly metamorphosing on the river*
> *And I am the bird, which when the spring comes*
> *Arrives in time to eat the mayfly.*
> *I am the frog swimming happily in the clear water of a pond,*
> *And I am also the grass snake,*
> *Who approaching in silence, feeds itself on the frog.*
> *I am the child in Uganda*
> *All skin and bones.*
> *My legs are still as bamboo sticks.*
> *And I am the arms merchant,*
> *Selling the deadly weapons in Uganda.*
> *I am the twelve-year-old girl, refugee on a small boat,*
> *Who throws herself into the ocean after being raped by a sea pirate.*
> *And I am the pirate,*
> *My heart not yet capable of seeing and loving.*
> *I am a member of the public bureau,*
> *Plenty of power in my hands,*
> *And I am the one who has to pay for the debt of blood to my people*

Dying slowly in a forced labor camp.
My joy is like spring,
So warm it makes the flowers bloom in all walks of life.
My pain is like a river of tears,
So full, it fills up four oceans.
Please call me by my true names,
So I can hear all my cries and my laughs at once,
So I can see that my joy and pain are one.
Please call me by my true names,
So I can wake up,
So the door of my heart can be left open
The door of com-passion.

Take a moment and allow that to flow through you to resonate.

Finding Belonging in a Spiritual Community

Now, going to the next part of that sentence, " I AM *is my shepherd*," the image of a sheep comes up. This can be heard as the voice of a sheep that is part of a flock. The sense of belonging to a flock can give assurance, that one is not alone, that one belongs to a community wherein one may find support.

Some of us, perhaps, are already fortunate enough to belong to a group where we can support one another, sitting together as a sangha, or practice community. Or perhaps we belong to a church or a religious community, which is certainly a very powerful way of finding companions along the way. Regardless, the invitation of this practice is to understand that our smaller sangha is also something we are called to see in the light of the global sangha, the global connection of each and every being. The small groupings that we find do not have to be dispersed, and we do not have to deny them. We find support in an open-ended grouping that we are called to cultivate. And these small circles are connected to other small circles with other expressions of what bonds them together so that we do not exclude one another but see ourselves as a part of a global sangha. The point of connection to every group, to every person, to every being is in hearing the resonance of that phrase, I AM is my shepherd. It is the I AM that guarantees my belonging to that universal flock, whereby I can find companions along the way in all beings; every being can be my teacher; every being can be my companion. Let us continue to hear that dimension of this I AM as enabling us to belong to the connected universal community of beings.

There have been spiritual communities who hold prayer-led meetings with a concern for the deteriorating ecological situation. There has been a series of meetings in different places toward the formation of a sangha of all beings, or toward a universal sangha, calling all beings together, people from various religious backgrounds and also including the animals and trees, a gathering of the universal sangha to look at our state of affairs, and to see what we can all do together to achieve wholeness and healing. There is a sense of wanting to see the whole earth as our sangha and that each and every being on this earth from the different species and different human cultural circles and cultural backgrounds can have a contribution in making this universal sangha one that truly goes toward a sense of wholeness rather than the situation that we have today in which nations are divided against other nations, ethnic groups are set against other ethnic groups, people, individuals, and families are set against one another, and those who have lord it over those who have not.

In a situation in which we humans see ourselves in opposition to one another, and human beings are set in opposition to nature and to the natural habitat, in which one's identity is set up against that of others, we see the result in the destruction and the deepening woundedness of our earth community. We are called to take a turnabout in direction, and this call for a universal sangha is a call for a transformation of our way of seeing ourselves in relation to everything, a change in direction in the way we are living in our earth community.

In the light of that call, if we see that the flock we belong to is the community of all sentient beings, then the concern for the entire flock will naturally be nurtured and cultivated in our hearts, and we will be drawn to offer our whole being toward the healing of that universal flock.

As we are able to affirm with the psalmist, I AM is my shepherd, we also know by implication that we belong to a flock, that is, in a community of others who are also cared for by the same shepherd. Here though is a possible pitfall to watch out for. Our sense of aloneness in this world often makes us want to find a kind of belonging to a group. We want to be in the in-crowd, even from grade school on to middle school, to high school, to belong to the cool crowd and not be among the nerds. That sense of wanting to belong is deeply rooted in us. If we do happen to be among the fortunate ones who are included among those who are regarded as cool, the tendency is to divide a line between ourselves and those who are not. That already causes a rift in the midst of our being. If we find a sense of belonging in an organization, like a church, the tendency there, the pitfall there, is to look at those others outside that flock as not part of us anymore.

We are called to see through this and not hold on to the false scaffoldings that finite groupings provide for us and realize that we are part of a flock, precisely because we are part of, and are connected with, all that is included in this I AM. Whatever belongs to I AM, that is our flock. And if we really realize the implications of that, we can ask, is there anything that is outside of that? If we look around us, the trees, the dried leaves, the ground, the dogs, the cats, the stars the clouds, is there anything outside of I AM?

We are given the assurance, *I AM is my shepherd*, and I am able to realize that I belong not to some elite group that excludes others, but to a community that includes and embraces everything that exists in this entire universe. I am part of this universe, and I belong, just as each and every thing in this entire universe belongs, to all that is embraced in this I AM. With this realization, I see that each and every thing in the universe becomes a gift to everything else. I am also a gift that is given to everything, as I find my sense of connectedness with everyone and with everything. And everything in the universe is also a gift that is given to me. In saying "I AM is my shepherd," I come to see that I belong to a flock tended by that same shepherd. And "the flock" is no other than the entire universe, where each and every thing that exists also finds its place and sense of belonging.

My day job consists in teaching at a United Methodist theological school whose founding inspiration is John Wesley. John Wesley, among his many writings, is known for having remarked that "the world is my parish." He was an itinerant preacher and everywhere he went, without considering any territorial boundaries, he welcomed everyone in his heart and simply offered the Good News of salvation as he himself experienced it and as he received it.

That is the kind of universal heart that we are invited to cultivate in hearing the sentence "I AM is my shepherd." In the way that we find ourselves belonging to that community tended by that shepherd, we are also invited to take on the role of shepherd for the whole flock. As we hear and become rooted in the phrase I AM, we are called to be co-creators and co-healers. As we receive the healing power that is given to us, we are also called to be instruments of healing. Francis of Assisi prayed, "Lord, make me an instrument of thy peace." As we open our eyes to the source of peace and the gateway to peace that exist in our connectedness through the gateway of I AM, we are empowered to become instruments of peace in this world. How we will do that in our own contexts and in our given situations is something we need to discern individually, and in groups collectively wherever we are. Those are some of the dimensions we can hear as we recite this first phrase "The Lord is my shepherd; I AM is my shepherd."

I Know Only Contentment

The next phrase begins with *I shall not want.* I AM is my shepherd, I shall not want. This is a very powerful invitation to ask ourselves what it is that I want. In this life we find ourselves with so many needs, with so many wants. We continue to search for the pearl of great price in our lives. Just to offer a pointer, in Japan there is a famous temple in Kyoto named Ryōanji. There is a small well that is constructed so that it is surrounded by four characters that together spell out the message, "I know only contentment." Each of the four characters for "I," "know," "only," and "contentment," as written in the Japanese ideogram has a part that can be represented as an empty space or a hole. And the four characters are written in an ingenious way whereby the empty space or hole in each of the individual characters is placed right in the middle of the entire diagram, and the other parts of each character are written from top right to bottom left, reading the four in clockwise order to make up a complete sentence, "I know only contentment."

The compounded ideogram that surrounds the well conveys this four-character message, "I know only contentment," and at the center of it all is the empty space. In short, it is that empty space that becomes the clue to whatever that contentment is all about. One may not be able to appreciate this fully without knowing how those Japanese characters are written, but the message inscribed around this well, where fresh water bubbles up continually, is a subtle hint as to where we may be able to find the source of that contentment that we seek in our lives, whereby we are able to exclaim the words of the psalm, "I shall not want."

"There is nothing I shall want," is another translation for this. There is nothing I shall want anymore, because I have emptied of all my attachments and clingings to this or that. Not only that, more fundamentally, there is nothing I shall want because I am now filled to the brim. Later on in the psalm, we will be able to exclaim, "My cup overflows." Where is that coming from, that which overflows from my cup? It is not only that I shall not want, that I no longer have to try to scrounge around for things to fill my cup, but it is brimming so that I am called to share what is in my cup with everyone else. How can we realize that situation whereby *I shall not want*? It is not so much a matter of "attaining" it—it is simply opening our eyes to the fact that we are already endowed with infinite treasures, bubbling up like fresh springwater from within our midst, in being just as we are.

That fundamental want, that "lack" that we feel from within, as we are thrown into this life as beings separated from our source and not knowing who we are, makes us clamor: "I want this. I want that." "I want a companion," or "I want material security," or "I want a good secure place for my retirement," and so on. Those are the things that we find wanting in our finite and temporal situation, and we see ourselves as needy beings.

As we ground ourselves, however, and hear that singular message, I AM, we realize our connectedness with all, and see how everything is embraced within that I AM. Our hearts are thus filled to the brim, in a way that we only want to share and give to others, more than wanting to take or receive from them. Looking back at that empty hole in the Japanese temple well, the message of that fourfold character, *I know only contentment,* comes home to us.

We are invited to see through these kinds of things that we tend to grasp and hold on to, and instead let go of them, and be able to see that beneath all of these temporal and secondary wants and needs is a deep, deep well, a well that is the source of living waters, the source of nourishment for all that we need in this life. This well invites each of us to dip into it, to immerse ourselves in it. Our practice of sitting in stillness enables us to see where the source of those living waters lies within ourselves. To find that source and have continual access to it every day of our lives enables us to exclaim, truly, *I shall not want.* Let us take that as our invitation to find that source of living waters right in our midst.

When that I AM is no longer just a concept or a sound but when it has truly penetrated one's whole being and when one's whole being is fully dissolved in that I AM, then there is nothing that needs to be done anymore; there is nothing that is left out. The whole universe and beyond is all there, in that I AM. Listen. This practice of sitting together in silence is simply a way of letting that I AM sink in and letting our whole being plunge into that I AM such that we are immersed in it, and there is nothing that we ever can want after that.

In Japan there is a poem learned by middle-school children that comes from the Confucian tradition, which goes as follows:

> *If I realize the Way in the morning*
> *I am ready to die at dusk.*

It is simply pointing out that this realization of the Way is our supreme goal in this life. The point of living in this life is to experience the Way and to embody the Way. Once you realize that Way, then you are ready to die. This does not mean that you literally die right then and there, but conveys a key point: now your life is no longer something that is spent seeking or grasping or wanting things, but it is now turned around and now offered to the whole world as gift, as a pointer of that Way for others. As one embodies that Way and continues to live it, one then becomes a beacon for everyone else. But one becomes so not in a self-conscious way, saying, "I have found it, so I am showing those poor others the Way." Rather, in simply in being who you are, you become a gift to the world, a gift to the rest of us. That is what can really ground us in true contentment. *I shall not want.*

Of course, we will still have many wants in terms of human needs. We will still need to have a livelihood that will enable us to feed our children and to continue living in society. We will still need to fulfill our tasks in our job. We will still need to meet up with our obligations, pay our taxes. Those human wants and needs will continue, but that phrase, *I shall not want*, is something that we can experience from deep within. Having experienced it as such, what more can I want? What more can I ask for? Everything is there. Everything else is simply just following up with whatever the situation calls for. Let us take that hint from that very first word and immerse ourselves in that. I AM.

All the Days of Our Lives

The rest of Psalm 23 is just an unpacking of that which is involved in encountering that I AM. When one has acknowledged I AM as the shepherd of one's life, when one has true belonging, not in a small, little group that is excluded or is set off from others, but that true belonging to all that I AM, one is now able to embrace each and every element in this universe, each and every being as one's very own. That true sense of belonging whereby we find ourselves connected with everyone is who we are.

> *I am able to rest in green pastures.*
> *I am guided in the waters of rest or stillness of waters.*
> *I am guided in those waters that are rest-*
> *ful, through restful waters I am led.*
> *My soul is restored.*
> *I will be led in the path of righteousness,*
> *Even though I walk in the valley of darkness,*
> *I will not fear evil,*
> *For you are with me.*
> *Your rod and your staff, they comfort me.*
> *You have set a table before me in the pres-*
> *ence of my enemies, my oppressors.*
> *You have anointed my head with oil.*
> *My cup overflows.*

That is who we are as we experience I AM. The deep sense of peace and joy and gratitude bubbles forth from our very being without fanfare, touching everyone we meet in our daily lives.

Goodness and mercy, *tov va hesed*, refers to that absolute goodness that is referred to in Genesis that announces, *God saw that it was good.* It is that sense of absolute Good, an affirmation of the Good that we exude from our being as created in God's image. Together with that, we have *hesed*, that outpouring of God's compassion, that agape that embraces all in an outpouring of love and grace,

That will surround me all the days of my life,
And I shall dwell in the house of I AM to the length of my days.

The psalm illustrates what the realization of that I AM effects in our lives. The image of green pastures where all beings can rest and find nourishment together brings up another scene in another passage in the Hebrew scriptures where the lion lies together with the lamb (Isa. 11:6), which we will consider a little later in connection with a subsequent passage. How can those two beings, which are natural enemies, lie together in peace?

We are invited to sit at a table where we share with those whom we would call enemies but who are really not enemies. They are a part of us as we arrive in and come home to I AM. That I AM is something that we can identify with each and every person we meet. We feast together in that place where we can celebrate our being together. There are such events in this world. That is precisely what gives us all hope. To be human is to be capable of that kind of celebration. This enables us to celebrate. It is good to be alive. It is good to be because there is that capability to go across boundaries and affirm one another. Those are the green pastures.

Through restful waters I am led. "Still waters" is another translation. Let us take the hint and continue to cultivate stillness in ourselves. As stillness becomes more palpable, we will see how nourishing it can be. The novelist Thomas Hardy describes human life as a desert with one or two oases. Here is the oasis that we are all invited to dwell in and take our nourishment from, that place of stillness where we can truly be grounded in I AM. You never have to leave that oasis, once you have discovered where it is. It is right here, where you are with each breath. It is an invitation to be there. All the nourishment we will ever need for our lives, through all the rough tumbles and through all the twists and turns that we will encounter—all the source of nourishment is right there, breathing in and breathing out, available to us.

I will be guided in the way of righteousness. This righteousness is in Hebrew *tsedek,* and in Greek it is *dikaiousune,* that which marks a person as "saved." This is the righteousness before God and before the entire community of human beings. But it is not a righteousness that proclaims itself with a sense of condemnation of others who are not righteous, but it is simply an affirmation of that which is most truly what each thing is and truly what one is. This is the way of being who one truly is.

In the East Asian tradition, the Way, the Dao, is held up as something that guides us in our living on this earth on three levels. It is understood to be the way of the cosmos, the way things are, the way of the universe. The second level is the way of nature, why the flowers bloom, why the trees stand tall, why spring takes over after winter and then summer comes and the autumn leaves and so on, the way of nature. The third level is the way that human beings are called to live in harmony with one another. If those three levels of the Way are integrated in our lives, then truly we will be at peace. From that angle, this phrase from Psalm 23, *I will be guided in the way of righteousness,* is an invitation for us to live in that Way.

Now, I would to take a hint from a koan in the Zen tradition that talks about the Way. What is the Way? How can we live that way in our lives?

In this koan, we see the Zen Master Joshu, who is known also for the *mu* koan described earlier, when he was still a young aspirant beginning to launch his spiritual journey. It is number 19 of the collection known as the Gateless Gate.

Joshu asks Master Nansen, "What is the Way?"
Nansen replies, "Ordinary mind is the Way."
Joshu asks, "How should I direct myself to it?"
Nansen replies, "If you direct yourself to it, you go against it."
Joshu asks, "But if I do not direct myself to it,
how will I know that it is the Way?"
Nansen replies, "The Way is beyond knowing and not know-
ing. Knowing is delusion. Not-knowing is blank conscious-
ness. When you will have reached the Way beyond doubt, you
will find that it is vast and wide as the great firmament. How
can it be talked about on the level of right and wrong?
With that, Joshu came to a sudden realization.

What is meant by this, "Ordinary mind is the Way"? Nansen is telling the young man Joshu, an earnest spiritual seeker,
Joshu, that he does not have to do anything special or out of
the ordinary to realize the Way. Get up in the morning, wash
your face, take your breakfast, go to work in the fields, get
tired, wipe the sweat from your brow, come back for lunch,
take a rest, and come back again. Laugh, cry, dance, sit, sleep.
All of that is the Way.

Let us take a hint from that. When you ask, what is my
True Self? Or, who am I? the answer is all there, in each and
every event of our day-to-day lives. What you are looking for
is *right there*, as you do all of those things you do, just as you are.

"Ordinary mind is the Way." Joshu, understanding that con-
ceptually, asks, "If it is a matter of just doing what I am already
doing, how should I direct myself toward it then, if that is the
Way?" Nansen replies, "If you direct yourself toward it, you
go against it." If you consciously put up for yourself a goal
or objective that you wish to attain, and then direct yourself
toward that, then you are actually separating yourself from it
by doing so. Joshu is startled, seeing a paradox here. I want

to know the Way. I want to live the Way. I want to give my entire being toward discovering that Way, and yet you tell me, "If I should direct myself toward it, I go against it." How do I deal with that? He is left at an impasse here. What is the Zen Master Nansen pointing to here? If we think that there is a Way "out there" that we can pursue, and so we try to pursue it, then in that very thought we are already dividing ourselves, separating ourselves from the True Way. That very thought of wanting to attain the Way becomes a hindrance to realizing it.

In short, Nansen is saying, "Do not pursue it as if it were something in front of you, outside of you, separate from you." This is like a dog who sees its own tail and tries grab it with its mouth. In trying to do so, it would just go around in circles forever, never getting to what it desperately wants.

So Joshu again, in his simple heart and straightforward way, asks, "But then how can I know that it is the Way, if I do not direct myself toward it?" Nansen's reply is true to form as a Zen Master. "The Way is beyond knowing or not knowing. It is as vast and wide as the empty firmament. How can you pursue it in terms of knowing and not knowing, of right and wrong?" There Nansen assures Joshu, it is a not matter of your pursuing or not pursuing. The Way is simply being *as you are.* Joshu awakens and realizes this.

When we seek to embody the Way in our lives, we are counseled not to think that the Way is out there that we can pursue given enough effort and given enough meditation time. We are assured that we are already in the midst of that which we are pursuing earnestly with our whole heart and mind. The Way is in you! This is also a title of a book published by the Jesuit priest Niklaus Brantschen, who is also a Zen Master: *The Way Is in You.*[1]

---

[1] Nicklaus Brantschen, *Der We gist in Dir* (Zurich: Benziger, 1996).

But do not think that it is "in you" as opposed to something "outside you." It is, again, not that kind of thing that is separating the outside from the inside. You are right there in the midst of it, so just open your eyes. It is like a fish asking, where is the water? Just relax and swim, not even thinking of swimming, just be as you are and there the Way is fully manifest. That is the hint we are receiving from this koan.

I will be guided in the paths of righteousness. I AM will be my guide, in walking the path of righteousness, the eternal way, the way of the universe, the way of nature, the way of human living that is conducive to peace and harmony within myself and with the entire cosmos. How will I be guided? Who will be my guide? *Thy rod and thy staff will comfort me.* That rod and staff—we might be tempted to think of them as an outside goad, and if we go the wrong way, well we might be hit and told to straighten up. But again it is not that kind of external chastising to which this is pointing. It is that inbuilt voice that tells us what the Way is all about. It is the still, silent inner voice that assures us we are on the right path. In the Catholic tradition, we call it conscience. This is what guides us also in our human reflection on how to live a moral life. What we call conscience straightens us up and tells us, in an immediate and intimate fashion, how we are to live, and not go astray. This voice of conscience is in each and every one of us. You will know what you are to do and how you are to respond: just listen to that inner voice.

Again, in the New Testament scriptures, "When you are placed before tribunals and asked about important things, do not be anxious about preparing what to say in those tribunals, because the Spirit will guide you" (Luke 11:12). That which is in you already, which has been guiding you all the way, which drew you out of nothingness into being, that same power will let you say what you need to say. Let us trust that it is already in us. Our way of coming back to that is simply to come back to the here and now, where the voice of I AM is most audible and palpable in our lives.

Even though I walk in the valley of darkness, I will not fear evil. This does not mean that no harm will come upon me, nor upon those I love. We have a world where there is so much violence going on, so much hatred, and so much conflict. Evil is a fact. It hurts many people. It is evil that 20,000 children die of hunger-related causes every day on this earth. It is evil that causes forests and many green spots to be leveled off and gradually to be turned into deserts or desolate spots; it is evil that causes our earth to be piled up with toxic waste. It is evil that causes all the pains of the children in places of conflict, in places where people have been uprooted from their homes and driven to places they know not and put in uncertain living conditions. That is the fact we are confronted with from day to day: our earth is gravely wounded; evil is everywhere. What the psalm is saying is not that there will not be evil, but "even though I walk in the midst of the valley of darkness, I will fear no evil." The evil that is all around us, I will not fear, in the way that paralyzes me so that I am unable to act in front of it. No, the Way will guide us as to how we are to comport ourselves in the midst of this violence and evil; the Way will enable us to experience deep inner peace in the midst of all this. In the midst of danger, in the midst of conflict, we will know where we stand; we will know where to step and how to respond, guided by the Way, guided by that rooted-ness in I AM. It is like being in the eye of the storm, where throughout all the turmoil and violence around us, we will know that place of peace. We will not shy away from the turmoil but will be in the midst of it and offer that place of peace to all. If we have found that place of peace, where we are one with I AM, then that is what we can offer to the world, a gift of peace, a peace that no one can take from anyone who has truly been grounded in it.

You will set a table before me in the presence of my enemies. It is continuing hope. It is a continuing scenario that draws us on, to have that kind of table where we can feast with our so-called enemies, and we can celebrate our lives together.

Here I am reminded of another very graphic scene from a film called *Places in the Heart*, directed by Robert Benton. Sally Field stars in this film depicting life during the depression era in 1930s in a town in the southern United States. The Sally Field character is a housewife named Edna, married to the sheriff of the town, with small children. We see them as they go about their daily lives as a happy family together. Then a tragedy ensues. The sheriff is called out one night while they were having dinner. There is gunfire. The next scenes show the sheriff dead, accidentally killed by a young black boy of the area, named Wylie, who happened to be playing with a gun. The townspeople gather together in anger, pick up the boy, and lynch him, drag his body from a truck and show it all around town. There are sad and grisly scenes all over. Then the film goes on to depict Edna continuing on with her life, having lost her husband, trying to raise her children as best she can, struggling to save and maintain their family farm, which she is able to do with the help of a blind man and a former drifter who becomes a loyal farm hand. Toward the end of the film is the scene I would like to highlight here. It is a surreal scene, where we see all the characters seated in pews in church, and we see the face of each character focused on one by one. There is Edna with her children, and also her husband the sheriff sitting there side by side. And then beside him, there is Wylie, the black boy who had killed the sheriff, who had been tortured and lynched by the mob, also sitting there in his best Sunday clothes. We then see the faces of the different townspeople who participated in the lynching, also sitting there on the pews. They are passing a plate full of Bread, the

Eucharist, giving it to the next person, one by one. The film ends with Wylie greeting the sheriff, "Peace of God."

This last scene of the film invites us to a contemplative moment. The different individuals who have appeared in the film, both living and dead, are shown in this scene, sitting in church, passing the Bread from one to the other. We see them here in their Sunday best, but we also recognize in each person the particular struggles, their words and their actions toward one another, as constituting all that they are. The woundedness that marked their particular lives on earth is borne by each one of them even as they sit there, and all of that is shown on their faces as we contemplate them just sitting there in the pews. And all of that is embraced, and accepted, and forgiven as they take the Bread together, in Eucharistic thanksgiving. It is a surreal scene indeed, but it is inviting us to consider what that "feast before one's enemies" entails. It offers a vision in which we can celebrate one another and overcome the opposition that pits us against each other in this limited and finite existence of ours. We are invited to see that as the scenario into which we are all called to participate, where truly the lamb can sit beside the lion (Isa. 11:6) in peace and harmony, where we can feast together with those we had considered our enemies, and celebrate our being together.

This moving scene gives us a glimpse of the *kin-dom* that we are talking about here, that kin-dom that is in our midst, which we are invited to see and activate in our own individual lives. *Thy kin-dom come. Thy will be done on earth as it is in heaven.* That which is beyond, heaven, comes home on *this side* where we are and where we conduct our lives, in a way that becomes manifest and embodied right here. Again the message for us is this: "Do not look hither and thither." We need not try to grasp it somewhere out there, outside of us, or in some distant future. The *kin-dom* is in our midst.

Only when each one of us has been able to cultivate that heart that is grounded in I AM, that embraces each and every one, no matter what their background, no matter who or what they are, as they are, can that take place. It begins right here, with us, as we are able to embrace each of us, especially those who irritate us at work or at home, especially those with whom we find it hard to get along, especially those who malign us with words or even threatening actions. If we relate back to them with the same animosity, then we prevent that scene from happening. It is in our hearts that we can allow that to happen as each of us takes down those barriers that separate humans or beings from one another. As we cultivate within us that home that can welcome all beings together in the same home, we come to the point of being able to feast with our enemies.

You have anointed my head with oil. The anointing with oil is an important image in Hebrew scriptures going into the New Testament because the word *messiah* means the Anointed One. If one reads it in this way, "You have anointed my head with oil," each one who is able to recite the psalm acknowledges with gratitude that "you have anointed my head with oil," not for any merit of mine, not for any good deeds that I have done as a reward, but in a gratuitous way, in a totally grace-filled kind of way: "You have anointed my head with oil, have filled me with every kind of blessing." Who is the messiah, the Anointed One? In your own special way, that is you, that is each and every one of us, and we will meet other anointed ones too, in our day-to-day lives. We will celebrate one another's being together. Hear this. That is you. I AM, that is you.

My cup overflows. That is something that we have already been able to hear and already connected with everything else that has been noted before. We are no longer leading a kind of life that is desperately seeking or wanting or grasping something that we think we don't have. Now, having found our place of peace, having come home, where we are connected with all that is, now my cup overflows with gladness and joy, and also overflows with compassion for all. As I open my eyes to the wounds of my fellow sentient beings, my heart goes out to them, seeking to be an instrument of their healing, of our healing together. My cup overflows; my heart overflows with that desire to be of help in some way or other, in the particular ways that I am able to.

Surely and goodness and mercy will follow me all the days of my life. Each moment of my life I will hear that affirmation. *And God saw that it was good* (Gen. 1:10–31). This is the goodness contained in each moment as we live our lives immersed in Divine Love. "It is so good for us to be here," as Peter exclaimed. It is that exuberance of the realization of that goodness, the acceptance of that affirmation, *You are good and absolutely so*, that can enable us truly to jump for joy and realize that there is nothing more that we can ever want in each moment of our lives. That goodness also outflows into compassion, that outpouring of grace, that outpouring of love that we receive when we know that we are affirmed by unconditional love.

We no longer need to seek love in different places, in the wrong places, because it is *right here* already given to us in abundance. *You are beloved, you are good, and you are absolutely loved and embraced, and unconditionally so.* That is the word that each of us so earnestly seeks to hear in our lives, because we may have been deprived of that feeling of being loved. As children, our parents may have been unable to express that love, although they may have loved us; they themselves may have been still immature and caught in their own personal struggles; they may not have been able to manifest love to us their children. And so we felt deprived of love, and we go through life seeking to be loved by others, seeking approval from others, as a psychological tendency that can be noted perhaps because of those factors in our upbringing. Hearing this affirmation, *You are my beloved,* gives us that total self-confidence to find our place in this world and to contribute to its healing: "You are loved; you do not need to go on seeking love anymore, but now it is your turn to give back that love to each and every one that you meet, all the days of your life."

And I shall dwell in the house of I AM, for the length of my days. That is the invitation, and the good news, that we are already there. Let us open our eyes to that fact, that we are at home, as we are immersed in I AM. But our mind just imagines all sorts of things, leading us astray. It is our task simply to bring our minds back to where we are already home. What we endeavor in this practice is to sit in a posture of stillness and breathe with awareness and let our minds simply be there with the breath. This is our way of coming home. As we are able to find that home and live in it and truly dwell in it and find our peace in it, we are able to open that home in hospitality, to welcome all beings and let all the birds of the air, all the animals of the forest, and all human beings in that home. Let us come home first and then know that home is open, something that we can open to each and every one.

Chapter Three

﹏﹏✦﹏✦﹏

The Treasure That Is You
(Matthew 13:44–46)

The kingdom of heaven is like when someone finds a treasure hidden in a field, and in great joy, buries it again, goes and sells everything in order to buy that field. Again, the kingdom of heaven is like what happens when a jeweler finds a really valuable pearl, and goes and sells everything in order to buy that pearl.

—Matthew 13:44–46

Is That All There Is?

Our consumer-oriented and consumer-propelled society keeps bombarding us with messages, saying, "You need to have this (item or product), otherwise you will be behind everybody else." I am led to feel that if I do not have that particular product advertised, then I am nothing, worthless, just a nobody. Or I am led to think that other persons are better

than I am because they have what I do not. We compare and
then feel inadequate in not matching up to the ideal set before
us. We feel insecure, unstable.

We thus go through life seeking and grasping and wanting to have more things, and wanting to have more power
over others, driven as it were by that inner insecurity we feel
because of these messages from the media that invade our
inner psyche. We go on pursuing one thing after another, and
if we don't get them, we are unhappy. And if we do happen
to get hold of what we were seeking, after a while we realize
it was not such a big deal after all, and we begin looking for
something else again. This is a vicious cycle that messes up our
lives—grasping and seeking for something that is not really
going to truly satisfy us.

Entering a silent retreat is to take up the call we hear from
deep within ourselves, and take another look at how I am
living my life right now. I ask myself, Is this way I am living
really what I want for the rest of my life? Is this really what is
important to me?

What are the kinds of pursuits that occupy my time and
energy and draw me from one direction to another? Peggy
Lee's famous song, "Is that all there is?" hits it right there. Are
there things in my life that I know from deep within that I
do not need to do, or need not pursue, or I do not need to
keep spending so much time on, and yet something just keeps
me doing them? I may know deep within that I need to just
let go of certain things in my life, to free myself, and thus be
able to give myself more to what my heart really calls me to,
but I am not able to do so yet. Are there such rumblings I am
hearing in my life?

If we give ourselves the leeway to stop and plumb the
depths of our inner being, we may be able to see and acknowledge these dissatisfactions more clearly. As we take a straight

look at them with inner composure, we may be led to say to ourselves, "I need to let go of this."

A man named Siddhārtha Gautama was in such a situation when he was in his late twenties, and he was able to brace himself to make what is now known in history as the Great Resolve. He followed his heart's yearning, leaving everything behind, and went out to seek the answers to the Big Questions that had been welling up in him. After six years of intense search that took him to try different kinds of spiritual practice, he awakened, found deep inner peace, and lived the rest of his life offering it to everyone else who came to him for guidance, so that they might also experience awakening as he did, and find peace for themselves, and in turn give their own lives for others. The rest is history.

What do I need to sell and let go of in my own life, so that I can take possession of that pearl of great price?

We need to ask ourselves: What is there that keeps me in this sense of inner instability, a sense of insecurity, of fragility, as I go on with my life? What holds me in that sneaking feeling that I am not fully grounded in my life? What is behind all this "dis-ease"? And as the question is asked with earnestness, then I am able to acknowledge that I am in a situation in which I seek something to make me complete, that I am not yet whole and fully myself, that I am insecure or unstable, that I am confused, and am lost. To acknowledge this state of being lost or being confused, or this uncomfortable state of not knowing, is an important stage that enables us to take stock of where we are, and be able to clear the way and set our gaze truly and firmly on what is important and how we need to go forward from there. As we recognize the fact of being lost or confused and in search, that becomes a goad to start what the parable invites us to do, namely to begin to dig and uncover that treasure in the field we are claiming for our own.

In so doing, we may recognize for example, that we seek something we can describe as a sense of being appreciated, valued, loved just as we are, just as I am. We may have grown up in an atmosphere wherein perhaps our parents did not give us a sense that they loved us, and so we were always seeking that love in some form or another. We come to realize that this was what drove us to this or that pursuit in life, that is, the inner need to find that assurance of being loved. We thereby recognize this drive in us that leads us to always seek but never find and never being satisfied. After thirty, forty, even fifty years, we are still in that state of seeking the true love that can truly satisfy our hearts.

If we recognize that as our own situation, we are invited to open our ears and listen anew from the depths. Let us take all of that confusion, all of that seeking and grasping, all of that sense of being lost, as our starting point, accepting ourselves as we are. Now let us simply come back to just being who we are, sit still, and in that stillness, open our hearts to listen from within. What is it that awaits to be heard? Who hears?

As noted earlier, Zen offers a methodical and systematic set of guidelines that allow us to listen from the depths of our being. It consists in keeping a straight posture, breathing in a regulated and attentive way, and letting our mind be silent, attentive to the here and now. These guidelines enable us to allow the treasure to manifest itself. Perhaps the term "digging" may be a little misleading because it is not so much digging but just letting the dust fall off, letting the gathered debris in our lives that prevents us from seeing the treasure be blown away. This methodical and systematic way of just being, just breathing in and breathing out, is our way of enabling that treasure that lies deep within us to emerge and become manifest.

In short, Zen gives us a very practical set of directives that may enable us to bring out that treasure in the full light of day and enable us to claim full ownership, and use it and spread it around to others also.

Digging for the Treasure

Again, as described earlier, the Zen tradition offers at least two different approaches for seekers to be able to uncover that treasure. One way is to *just sit*. The individual is enjoined literally to just sit, but not just sit in a slouching or in a haphazard position. One is given concrete guidelines on keeping one's legs in a way that one can sit with one's back straight so that one does not put undue pressure on one's legs. One then arranges one's whole body posture in a way that is conducive to stillness, and then one is enjoined to breathe deeply but naturally, letting one's mind simply be there without wandering all over the place. Initially, one follows the breath in its movement, inhaling, exhaling, inhaling again, and so on. One then lets the mind settle in this rhythm, and as one goes on, it becomes a matter of just "being there" with each breath, bringing the mind back whenever it goes elsewhere to follow a stray thought.

Appropriate posture, breathing, and silencing the mind are the three basic components of this mode of sitting. Being told to "just sit" is like being thrown into the water after being given the initial instructions on how to move one's arms and legs when in the water. "Just sitting" is the mode that is practiced in different Zen centers throughout the world, and this can also be regarded as the most advanced form of Zen practice, as one gets more and more proficient in it. It is a matter of just sitting, breathing in and breathing out, and enabling oneself to just experience the miracle of each breath and moment. This is the matrix that Zen offers to all of those who wish to partake of the fruits of this practice: this experience of just sitting, just being fully there, right here, right now.

The experience of just sitting flows out into the experience of just walking, when we are walking. In these meditative walks, we experience that pure movement of taking this step, taking the next step, taking a turn, taking the next step, and so on. Each movement is experienced just for what it is, as it is. That, again, flows out into the experience of just going back to the hall, just standing, and then just bowing before everyone, just going in single file to the dining room, just sitting on a chair, just taking the meal, and just standing up after the meal, just washing the plates and utensils. This practice opens us up to the idea of just this, so that in each moment, we are just there, doing just that. It is in those moments when we are just there that the treasure shines resplendent, the treasure that goes beyond the boundaries of chronological time that is restricted by the flow from the past to the present and going on toward the future. In the midst of this flow, we are enabled to take a glimpse of that *eternal now*, right there where we are.

Another approach that complements the approach of "just sitting" is the form of meditative sitting and considering a koan. In this mode, our noisy and restless mind is given something to hold on to, to help it stay focused so that it doesn't go all over the place. One just lets the koan be the focus of one's attention so that one can literally dig deep into one's own being, dig deep into one's subconscious mind. One's mind is not separated from one's whole being, but it enters the field where thinking and being are one. In that place where thinking and being are not separate, there is a revelation that can happen. That revelation is called *kensho*, in Japanese, seeing one's true nature.

One koan that many are familiar with is the koan *mu*, which we briefly noted earlier. One is enjoined to sit with the inscrutable word *mu* as one's guide to digging within the depths of one's being.

Once more, the koan goes like this.

A monk asks Zen master Joshu in all earnestness: "Does a dog have Buddha nature or not?"

Joshu answers, Mu.

That is it. The whole koan is in this brief exchange between the monk and Zen Master Joshu. Now the practitioner is to take that answer of Joshu as one's guide to going deep into the core of one's being, focusing on it while breathing in and breathing out. It thus becomes like a digging tool, which enables one to plumb the depths of one's mind and the depths of one's being, emptying out all extraneous and unnecessary things and going deeper and deeper into the heart of the universe. Like a laser beam, one enables *mu* to penetrate through the core of one's being and open what is there.

In that sense the practice of *mu* may be somewhat like the parable, whereby the merchant sells all that he has to be able to buy that field and make it his own. In breathing in and breathing out, one is enjoined to set aside all thoughts, set aside all attachments, set aside all clinging and simply be taken up by this Mysterious Event of breathing in and breathing out, and going more deeply into that divine darkness.

And as one moves into that dark place and becomes attuned to it, without grasping or being anxious, and one is able to trust that darkness, and accept it, one is able to dwell there and find peace and stillness. In that darkness, which you might call a deep darkness of the soul, "deep down things," to borrow an expression from the poet Gerard Manley Hopkins, somehow, something begins to dawn. It could be like an experience of any one of us, thrown into a room where the doors are shut and it is totally dark. We look for the switch and we cannot find it. At some point, we just stop our struggling and seeking, and just sit there in patience, in stillness. As we sit there, somehow our eyes become accustomed to the darkness and little by little, the room becomes visible in a gentle glow, and before we know it, everything is clear. We know that we are in a place that is safe, and we know that we are in a place where we can relax. It is home.

It is a matter of getting used to that divine darkness so that we do not seek something else outside of it, so that we do not seek some extraneous light to save us from our struggle, but we simply trust that we are already there, where we need to be. That is one way that this treasure can be unearthed, not so much by our efforts of getting something that is in there but by our trust that we are already where we need to be. We need simply to sit still and let that stillness be the locus wherein the treasure manifests itself. That is the way of unearthing the treasure with a koan.

There are other koans that can be used that are deemed by the teacher to fit certain practitioners more than others. That is just one example of one of those entry koans that are offered to those seeking with such intensity that they need that kind of instrument.

At this point, let me whisper to you a secret. What hint can we get from what the Gospels say here? *I will utter things which have been kept secret from the foundation of the world,* as the parable noted. Here's the secret you might be able to discover for yourself, as you undertake the journey down deep within: the surprising discovery that treasure *is the field* itself!

The "treasure" need not be some dazzling experience in our lives that will enlighten us and solve all our problems. It can be just a quiet experience that brings us to the realization that our entire life itself, lived from moment to moment, in everything that it entails, is itself the treasure this parable is talking about. Right from the moment we are born, to this present moment, until the time we cease our biological existence, that entire reality, "the works"—that is the treasure. All the elements in this life of ours are interconnected in one wondrous whole.

To use another image from the Buddhist context, it is like a Net of Indra. It is an infinite net, and each eye of that net is like a jewel, and each jewel reflects all the others. That is the capsule of my entire life, as I breathe in and breathe out, here, now. As we open our eyes to that treasure, we know that that capsule reflects all the other moments of our lives also.

Our life is right here. In theological language, this may be called *realized eschatology*, the last things, the ultimate things, manifest right here and now. We are able to reclaim the things of our lives, all the twists and turns, all the nooks and crannies, all of those things that we did not think we wanted to have happened—they are all reclaimed and acknowledged as treasure. Sitting still is our acceptance of the invitation to let that treasure be acknowledged. But if you are still seeking something else, or if our minds are preoccupied with some other endeavors, then we will not be disposed to being able to recognize that treasure right there where it is showing itself right before us.

That is why a retreat, an opportunity to sit and just be, and just walk and just eat and just rest and just view the things around in a state of peaceful tranquility, is really a privileged time, a time of grace, and a locus wherein we are able to go beyond the boundaries of our limited experience in linear time and local space.

Let us take the opportunity to let this treasure be manifest just for what it is in our simple activities of just sitting, breathing in and breathing out, walking simply and slowly, going back, taking a walk, patting the dog. All of these little actions and little events are what makes up the *kin-dom*. I take this word "kin-dom" (and not the more conventional "kingdom") in a deliberate way that was suggested by the late Latina mujerista theologian, Ada María Isasi-Díaz, who noted the patriarchal overtones of "kingdom." Rather than attaching an unnecessarily hierarchical and patriarchal image to what we seek earnestly with our whole hearts and our whole being, Ada María Isasi-Díaz suggests that we should envision it not so much as a "kingdom," but as the kin-dom of God: this is the place where we, all of God's creatures, are recognized as kin to one another. It is that reality in which you and I and all sentient beings and all of creation can discover one another as intimately interconnected in divine love, truly kin to one another.

To realize the kin-dom is also to realize the treasure that I am an integral embodiment of that kin-dom, and to realize the gift that has been uniquely given to me. It is thereby to realize that I am also a gift that I am invited to give to the rest of my kin, that is, to all beings. We are invited to sit still, and let this fact be manifest: the precious and irreplaceable infinite treasure that is myself, in wondrous interconnectedness with the entirety of creation.

Really, I have little more to say than that, that is, to confirm that invitation for each and every one of us. The point here is not to "get" anything, not to "achieve" anything, but simply to allow ourselves to be, and let the fullness of that be-ing be manifest and experienced to the full, that we may indeed realize "what has been there hidden from the foundation of the world" (Matt. 13:35), revealed to us right here and now.

The Treasure Was There All Along

Let us continue considering the parable of the treasure hidden in the field, and the pearl of great price. If you ask me what they are all about, the most direct answer I can give is this: it's about you. It is about each and every one of us. It is about each and every sentient being in this universe. Here is another way of saying it: YOU ARE the treasure in that field. At the same time, you are the field, in which the treasure is hidden.

To get another angle and perhaps to better taste it, I would like to take a Buddhist perspective on this parable of the treasure in the field, or the pearl of great price, and just chew on a few suggestions from a Buddhist chant, Hakuin's Song of Zazen.

Hakuin was a Zen monk of the seventeenth or eighteenth century in Japan, and he is credited with having revived the Rinzai school of Zen in this period when it was in a state of decline or of ritualism and formalism. He gave it new life with his own experience and his practice and with the way he lived the life of Zen. He also discovered a lot of medicinal concoctions. He was sickly when he was a young man, and so he had to struggle with his own health, which led him to a sense of impermanence, and thereby to seek a form of spiritual practice that would also be conducive to his health. As he engaged in his practice of Zen, at the same time he tried to look for different ways to heal his own physical ailments. He is said to have been adept in diverse kinds of medicinal herbs and was able to offer them to people who sought help from him. He wrote some treatises on medicinal arts.

One of the things that he is credited with is the well-known Song of Zazen. This is continually chanted in Zen temples and Zen communities all over, not just in Japan but also in different translations throughout the world. This is the pointer we will take to help us in uncovering what the parables convey to us. I would like to go through some of these lines and call our attention to some of the precious nuggets that may lead us to that discovery of that treasure we seek.

From the beginning all beings are Buddha.

This is a proclamation of a matter of fact. There was not a time when we were not Buddha. What is a Buddha? It is not a divine being to be worshipped or some super-entity out there. It is simply one who is awakened to one's true nature and in being so awakened is thus truly free to be and to live as one is. This awakening to one's true nature is also an awakening to one's interconnectedness to all other beings, enabling one to regard all beings intimately as kin, and thereby able to live with a heart of compassion for all.

What this first line proclaims is that YOU are Buddha. And YOU are the pearl of great price. YOU are the treasure in the field. What are the implications for our way of living life from day to day, for our families, our workplace, and so forth? We are invited to digest and chew on this and let it dissolve into our whole being so that we are able to experience its implications and be an awakened one. What does being an awakened one entail, and what does it involve in terms of the way we live our ordinary lives? We will return to that a little further on, but now we go on to the next couple of lines.

Like water and ice—without water, no ice, outside us no Buddha.

Water and ice are just different forms of the same thing. Ice is a solidified form of water, and when it gets to the right temperature, it melts and comes back with its original nature, that flowing and very freely adjustable substance called water. Sometimes our Buddhahood, the treasure in us, gets hardened and becomes a little less flexible, or it becomes stuck on a corner. That is what we need to loosen up, so that it can come back to its original flowing and free nature. Perhaps the practice of sitting and breathing in and breathing out is what enables that ice, that we have become, to melt a little and to become more like who we are. Take this practice as simply a way of letting our hearts melt a little bit, to recapture who we are originally. How near the truth, yet how far we seek. It is right there under our noses. It is right there, more intimate to us than we are to ourselves, as Augustine noted about the presence of God in his life. God is more intimate to me than I am to myself. Let us hear that message and thereby be assured. It is not somewhere outside that you can grasp. We do not have to pay the right price or exert the right effort. It is not because of our efforts that it will become manifest, but perhaps, in many ways, it is in spite of our efforts. Let us take that to heart, and let it become manifest in the simplest way, as we listen in the stillness.

This passage reminds me of something that happened when I was on my way to Sand Springs, Oklahoma, for the annual Zen retreat at Osage Monastery a few years back. From previous years, I had been used to having one of the sisters of the monastery meet me at the baggage claim area, to lead me to the airport parking lot where the monastery car was. I was always glad to see a figure in white, either Sister Pascaline or another sister, standing there to meet me where I was to pick up my bag. This time, I was told that Helen Cortes, who regularly manages the logistical and other details for the retreat to help the sisters at the monastery, and who had driven ahead from Dallas, was to meet me at the Tulsa airport to drive me to the monastery. Coming down to the baggage claim area, I looked around, and saw no sign of Helen. Five and then ten minutes passed, and still no Helen. I thought maybe she had got delayed in traffic. So I took out my cell phone and called, and after one ring, she answered, and said, "I'm right here."

"But where are you? I cannot see you."

She responded, "I'm right here. Look!"

I thought she must have been in another baggage claim area around the corner of the same airport hall, so I walked around to look for her there. I went down the stairs and looked to the other side and looked all over, and still no Helen. So I called her again on the cell phone and asked, "Where are you?" Again her response was, "I am right here." I looked around, left, right, behind, in front again, but could not see her.

"But really, where are you?"

"I am right here! Look at me!"

I did not realize that when she said, "I am right here," she was in her car outside waiting for me to come out, looking at me from her car window through the glass pane of the airport hall. I could have seen her in her car if I had looked in her direction, but my mind was fixed on the idea that Helen was standing around the baggage claim area, so I kept looking for her there, and thus could not see her, though she was right across the glass pane looking straight at me. How near the truth, yet how far we seek! My mind was fixed on the thought that Helen, just like the sister who would usually pick me up in previous years, should be standing around the baggage claim area. I missed the point entirely, even though she kept assuring me over the phone, "I am right here, right in front of you!"

What we are looking for, the treasure that will make us rich for many lifetimes, is right there before us, in front of our eyes. If we are harboring some idea in our heads about where it might be, expecting it to be according to that idea of ours, we will be missing it. The only way is to be present, listen with our hearts in the stillness, with full attentiveness to each here and now, and open our eyes, so we can see. As Augustine suggests, it is more intimate to us than we are to ourselves.

Hakuin tells us that it is like someone already immersed in water who keeps on complaining, "I'm thirsty." We are already in the midst of water. We have everything that can fill us to the brim and more, to overflowing, and yet we do not realize it. So we cry out, "I'm thirsty; I want to drink," not realizing that we are right there, where the source of all our nutrition and the source of all of our joy is waiting for us to be discovered.

Like the son of a rich household wandering poor on this earth, we endlessly circle the six worlds.

That's us too. This is a reference to a story that is found in the Lotus Sutra, one of the well-known and highly influential scriptures of Mahāyāna Buddhism. In this story there was a young man of a very rich household who tells his father and mother that he would like to go out and venture into the world, to see what the world is like, and journey through far-off places for an indefinite time. The night before he goes off, the mother takes a precious wish-fulfilling jewel, one of those mythical jewels in the lore of South and East Asia and India, which grants its holder whatever one may wish. She takes this jewel and sews it on the back of the collar of the coat he was going to take for the journey. So he goes off the next morning and bids good-bye to his parents. He is given enough provisions and enough money for a year. But his journey continues beyond a year, and his provisions are exhausted; his money is spent. Bereft of resources in a far-off land, he does not know where to go or what to do. He goes wandering from village to village, seeking something to eat. He becomes emaciated and hungry and in tatters. Through all this, he still kept on his coat. One evening, when he was lying down, it was a little cold and put on his coat as he lay on the straw mat, and he felt a lump near his neck. He takes the coat, examines it, and finds something hard around the collar area behind the neck, and lo and behold, the rest you can imagine. He finds the wish-fulfilling jewel, and is thus able to use it to obtain whatever he wanted in provisions, and other kinds of need. It is only now that he realizes that it had been with him all the time.

At this point in the story, he realizes that now he is able to continue in his journey and go wherever he wants. Eventually, he comes home, and thanks his parents for having provided him with all that he needed.

This is like us: we do not realize that the source of our treasure is right here, and we miss it. We think that we are in need. I am alone, or I am destitute, or I want this or that, not realizing that all we could ever want has already been given to us. This is a parable that is often put in parallel with another parable in the New Testament, the parable of the prodigal son. We do not need to go into the detailed comparisons here. The point here is that, all the riches we need are being given to us, so let us open our eyes and check our collars or look around us, look within us, to see what we might find there.

The "six worlds" is a Buddhist phrase for the six realms of being. These realms begin with the hell-dwellers, those who are in a state of alienation from others and have chosen that state of alienation. They have rejected the companionship of others. They have chosen to be by themselves and have chosen to wallow in their selfish, self-centered world rather than be in any kind of relationship or open themselves to anybody else. In this world, there is self-induced suffering because people are just caught up in their own selves. In the Buddhist context, hell is not an eternal state, but it is one of those states of life that you fall into if you are so self-absorbed that you get stuck in that way of life and see nothing beyond your own little self. If you live in a way that is in accordance with that state, namely if you live selfishly, if you close off everyone from your own little world, then it is like creating your own little hell. There are people who consign themselves to hell in that way. That is the first of the six realms. Hell does not have to be fire and brimstone and all of those images of torture and suffering. The torture there is in the loneliness and the alienation that one experiences in not being connected with the rest of the sentient beings. It is something that one imposes on oneself if one's life is centered on one's ego and if one sees everything else from the narrow perspective of that ego.

The next world is the realm of the hungry ghosts. These are beings that roam throughout the world and throughout the universe trying to grasp for things because they are driven by incessant hunger, an incessant inner need. They may need or want for material things or for fame or possessions, or recognition, and so on. Whenever they meet somebody, they always think, what can I get out of this person? They always present themselves as needy, and their thoughts, words, and actions are always driven by that incessant need. That is the world of the hungry ghosts. In some Buddhist cultures, the existence of hungry ghosts roaming all over is taken literally. There is a custom among devoted Buddhists whereby, before taking a meal together, people would take a small morsel of food out of the plate from which they are about to have their meal, and place it in a receptacle set aside for the hungry ghosts. It is a symbolic gesture of sharing whatever blessings of food we have. We offer it to those who seek that kind of nutrition in ways unseen to us. It is a gesture of solidarity with all those beings who are hungry or are in need. If we go about our lives driven by an inner need that we may not be able to name but we know is always consuming us, making us always take on a mode of grasping or grabbing or seeking attention or seeking this or that, we are hungry ghosts.

The third level of being is that of the fighting or malignant spirits. These are the beings who always have a chip on their shoulder, always trying to pick a fight. They always need to be ahead of everybody else. They always want to compete and win. They may have a grudge against others and want to pick a fight, or they may just want to assert their superiority over others by controlling them. These are called ashuras, divinities who have fallen from the highest realm due to this incessant drive to compete and to win, and are "demoted" to a lower level of being in the six worlds.

On the fourth level are the animals. These are those who are described as living according to their instincts and lusts, without control of reason. In the natural world, we have the dogs and the cats and so forth. They are the gentle ones, but the animals of a different form, namely the animals in us, can be much more destructive. They are the ones that thrive on drivenness. They are not so much motivated by a basic need but are propelled to actions that they tend to follow to an extreme. The animal in us always waits to pounce on something, and it would destroy whomever we would take on as a victim. But it also works in reverse. It can also destroy us.

The fifth level of sentient beings is that of human beings. Here we find the being that contains all of the previous rungs but also has in oneself a principle by which one can see all of these and can place them in balance, namely, under the control of one's reason and sense of goodness and righteousness. Thus one can live in a peaceful way, in a way that is compassionate. The human being is said to be the center point of the six realms of beings because it is as a human being that awakening can happen. All of the previous rungs are so wrapped up in their own little worlds that there is hardly a chance for true awakening. True Buddha-hood can come about in the form of a human being. Although by nature, we are all Buddha, still we are caught in an existential situation in which we are selfish, hungry and grasping, in a fighting mood, or driven by lusts and so on. A human being has the capacity to balance all of these and see through these in a way that can lead to awakening, to Buddhahood.

The rung above that would be the heavenly beings. These beings are supposed to be the superhumans who have the capacity to fly from one end of the universe to the other. They are the deva, the divinities in the Indian pantheon equipped with powers to be able to see through past lives. They are equipped with extrasensory perception, able to help others, if they want to. But they are all living in a world of pleasure and contentment, so they tend to want to stay there. They get attached to the world of pleasure and contentment, so they do not seek enlightenment. Maybe we are also in situations like that sometimes. When things are good and we have a great job, we are satisfied; the money flows in, and everything is well in our little world, so we do not need anything more, and we want it to stay like that. We are satisfied in our little middle-class contentment. That is the deva world, the world of the beings that tend to wallow in pleasure and contentment and tend to stay there and not go a step further.

These are the six realms that we can continually go around in circles in this life on earth. This Song of Zazen tells us that we endlessly circle the six worlds, unsatisfied, being miserable, and causing others to be even more miserable, even though what we seek, namely the genuine satisfaction that comes from realizing our true nature, which is vast and boundless, is right there before us. Still, because we get caught up in immediate things in our day-to-day lives, we can miss that reality entirely.

The invitation that Zen practice offers is for us to take a straight look at ourselves, letting go of all obstructions to truly see ourselves as we are. In doing so, our heart may open up and usher in that infinite treasure waiting to be recognized.

The cause of our sorrow is ego-delusion.

In whichever of the six realms we might find ourselves, ego-delusion gets in the way and prevents us from our realizing true bliss, true joy in our lives. As long as we are centered on our little selves, with the idea in our head of who we think we should be or who we want to be, we remain trapped in ignorance. Our ego-delusion is what makes us unable to realize that we are connected with all beings. We are caught in a particular form of ego-delusion, depending on whether we remain in the hell-realm, or in the realm of hungry ghosts, or of the fighting spirits, or of animals. In any case, we are trapped in the prison of our little ego that acts up in a particular way in these different realms. Even if we somehow find ourselves in the heavenly or deva realm, the ego remains deluded, in that the finite satisfactions received in this realm, whether it be the pleasures of the senses, or of the intellect, or other more sophisticated pleasures, tend to make us smug and want to wallow into those pleasures, not to see beyond them. We are thereby disabled from seeing the vast and infinite horizon that our true nature opens up to us.

From dark path to dark path, we wander in darkness. How can we be free from the wheel of samsara?

The wheel of samsara again refers to the six realms whereby we keep on turning and turning, being born and reborn in the different states, caught up in our ego-delusion. It is when it finally dawns on us that going around and around these realms leaves us truly dissatisfied that we begin to seek liberation. This is the emergence of the bodhi mind, the mind of awakening. How can we realize this true freedom of awakening? Our Zen cushion beckons us.

The gateway to freedom is zazen samadhi.

The gateway to freedom, the way to see through all of these things, the way to see through our ego-delusions, is through sitting in stillness, and dwelling therein, allowing it to open us to an infinite horizon.

Taking up this invitation, we engage in this practice of sitting in a formal posture of meditation, breathing in and breathing out, and listening in stillness. As we continue to deepen in that stillness, we may get a glimmer of the world that is beyond this limited scope that our phenomenal world offers us, a realm that is boundless and beyond our imagination. As we sit there in silence, the walls can come tumbling down, the walls that separate us from everything and everyone else. It can happen in just little incidents that enable us to see things in an entirely different light.

It can be through hearing a bird, and that bird tells us who we are, who "I AM." As the bird is truly heard, it is no longer a sound made by a bird on a tree branch "out there." As long as I think that I am hearing a bird that is an object out there separate from myself sitting here on a cushion, then I am still caught in my ego-delusion. But as we cultivate this samadhi, that pure and clear realm where there is simply breathing in and breathing out, and as we dwell in that stillness, then in the middle of that stillness, a grace-filled event may happen. A bird chirps. And if the moment is ripe, a transformation may occur. The chirp of the bird may be likened to a gentle leaf that falls on the surface of a clear lake. That gentle leaf that falls will make a small ripple, a round wave that will slowly, gradually, but eventually envelop the entire lake. The whole lake is now graced with that wave, which is moving through the whole lake. In that graced moment, that chirping of the bird is no longer a sound heard from out there, and is now a sound heard throughout the entire universe, enveloping everything into it. The answer to the question "Who hears?" becomes fully manifest.

Or it could be the bark of a dog. It could be the sight of a leaf on a tree visible from a window of the meditation hall. It could be an aching sensation in my knee. It could even be a mental image from the past, or from recent events that have happened in my life, that wells up on the horizon of my mind. That image can somehow become a trigger for a realization of something significant: an opening to an infinite horizon of connectedness with everything in the entire universe, an open field that contains each and every being that exists in this entire universe. In such a moment, the gateway to freedom opens.

The Infinite Is Here and Now

Another scriptural testimony from the Buddhist tradition may throw light on what we are talking about here, about the field itself being the very treasure we are seeking.

The Heart Sutra is a Mahāyāna Buddhist text composed in the early centuries of the common era, which offers a succinct expression of the world of enlightenment and what this consists of. It is chanted in Zen halls in different parts of the world and has served to open the eyes of countless practitioners to the reality that they seek as they engage in their practice of meditation. This scriptural text is about the wisdom of seeing things as they are, a wisdom which in turn flows into a heart of compassion for all sentient beings.

Its message can be summarized in this way: "Form is no other than emptiness; emptiness is no other than form." This is the succinct expression of all that enlightenment entails. What does this mean? "Form is no other than emptiness, emptiness no other than form." Form refers to anything and everything that exists, which can be perceived and with definite and measurable dimensions within the space-time continuum. It is what can be seen, heard, smelled, touched, tasted, imagined— all those things around us that we are familiar with in our day-to-day lives. What do we see around us? We see the individuals around us, trees, dogs, or whatever creatures you may meet in your walk along the road, or the leaves—anything that you can touch, taste, and feel is form. And that includes not just those external forms that you see outside, but also what comes up in your mind, when you are sitting there, your memories of the past or your expectations of your future, and so on. All of those images or all of those events or all of those movements that come forth are "Form." That is the field wherein we live our lives. I identify with this individual that is the subject of "my consciousness," with my given name, which distinguishes "my" form from the myriads of other forms in the universe.

And now the Heart Sutra tells us, "Form is no other than Emptiness." What is this saying? First of all, it is very important to note that "Emptiness" here is not to be simplistically identified with "nothingness." In other words, this is not a statement reducing all existing things (what we described as "form" earlier) to a mere "nothing." Nor does it negate the value of human life—impermanent, mortal, fallible, laden with suffering and struggle though it may be. What then is this about?

The term that is translated as "Emptiness" comes from the Sanskrit word *śūnyatā*, an abstract noun derived from *śūnyam*, a word that can be translated as "zero." "Form is no other than Emptiness" is thus another way of saying "Everything that exists has the character of zero-ness." Now let us recall that "zero" in mathematics functions as the hub that is at the intersection of all positive numbers on the one side, and all negative numbers on the other. If we want to look for an image that can describe this, it is something like a lever, a fulcrum that holds the weight of the universe together in balance. It resonates very much with that fulcrum that Archimedes was talking about, when he famously said, "Find me a fulcrum (or lever) on which to stand, and I will move the universe."

"Emptiness" is thus a term used to refer to the point that is at the hub, at the ground of the universe, on which everything stands, which makes each and every thing in this universe precisely what it is in relation to everything else. The statement "Form is no other than Emptiness" may not be something we can figure out through a logical process, nor something we can readily explain didactically as what you may think I am trying to do here. Rather, I am using words here merely to invite everyone to place one's entire being onto that "Archimedean fulcrum," something like what the poet T. S. Eliot referred to as "the still point of the turning world."

As we sit in stillness, we are invited to simply entrust ourselves into each breath, inhaling, exhaling, with our heart open to the universe, eyes and ears and all senses open to everything around us, and let go of that controlling self-centered ego-consciousness that regards everything else as an "object" to itself. As we enter into the depths of that stillness and are truly able to let go of this ego-consciousness that separates us from the rest of the universe, we may find ourselves in that fulcrum, at that "still point of the turning world," and realize our True Face before all ages. The words of the poet may serve as pointers here.

> *At the still point of the turning world. Neither flesh nor fleshless;*
> *Neither from nor towards; at the still point, there the dance is,*
> *But neither arrest nor movement. And do not call it fixity,*
> *Where past and future are gathered. Nei-*
> *ther movement from nor towards,*

Neither ascent nor decline. Except for the point, the still point,
There would be no dance, and there is only the dance.

—*T. S. Eliot, Burnt Norton (1935)*

To come home to that still point is to realize our True Face, that Original Face that I Am "even before my father and mother were born," as the Zen koan goes—that is what recovering, discovering, uncovering the treasure is all about. Form, the field that we identify with our individual personalities, is no other than that Still Point that is our true home, which we seek and yearn for deep within our hearts, "more than the sentinel waits for daybreak" (Ps. 42), more than the one who stays on guard all through the night, and is now tired and weary, and waits longingly for the first light of dawn. As we nurture that longing in our sitting and breathing in and breathing out, let us simply be there, and let us be attentive each moment. As we do so, the words of scriptures may be fulfilled right before us, and we will find ourselves face to face with the treasure that we seek. It may dawn on us at any given moment, in and through any given particular item at hand—a tree in the front yard, the bark of a dog, the soft touch of a cat's fur, or the chirp of a bird, the sneeze of someone else in the room. If our hearts are fully open and attentive in that moment, that moment of grace, we will know without a doubt. And we will be overwhelmed with joy and gratitude.

"Form is no other than Emptiness." The realization of what this passage is pointing to entails a leap into an infinite horizon, right there at the place where we stand, or sit. But that is only to go part of the way. The passage continues: "Emptiness is no other than Form." We must follow where this boundless horizon leads us, to this next step. To borrow a phrase from *Toy*

Story, it is to leap to infinity, and beyond. This place "beyond" infinity is actually no other than this very place where we stand or sit or wherever we are, doing whatever we may be doing. It is a return home to that which is most familiar to us, and yet for some wondrous reason, again borrowing from T. S. Eliot, we know it for the first time.

> *We shall never cease from our exploration*
> *And the end of our exploring*
> *Will be to arrive where we started*
> *And know the place for the first time.*

> —*T. S. Eliot, Four Quartets*

Let me summarize what we have looked at in this section, taking our cue from scriptural passages from our Christian tradition seen in the light of Buddhist texts. This field that comprises the entirety of our human life is the place where each of us is called to open our eyes and claim our treasure, the treasure of our own True Self. This treasure is the experiential realization of who I AM as infinite and boundless, and also at the same time as intimately interconnected with everything that exists in this universe. We are able to realize this as we find our home in that "still point of the turning world." From this standpoint, all the pains, the joys, the concerns of the whole world are the very pains, the joys, the concerns I bear within myself. That realization thereby enables me to understand that the point of my life is simply to fully live this gift of who I AM, and offer it back to all as a gift, no longer just for my own satisfaction or fulfillment, but precisely as a gift of all that I am and all that I have, so that the treasure that is already there may be multiplied infinitely. This is how we can understand the realization of the kin-dom of God on this earth, as we all come to realize that we are kin to one another, in a most intimate kind of way, and live our lives accordingly.

Glowing Like the Sun

Let us now take another scriptural testimony, this time from the Letter to the Colossians ascribed to the Apostle Paul, to shed further light on this treasure that we are talking about.

> *God has given me the responsibility of serving his church by proclaiming his entire message to you. This message was kept secret for centuries and generations past, but now it has been revealed to God's people. For God wanted them to know that the riches and glory of Christ are for you Gentiles, too. And this is the secret, which is Christ in you, the assurance of his glory.*
>
> *—Letter to the Colossians, 1:25–27*

The word translated in English here as "secret" is *mysterion* in Greek, rendered as "mystery" in other versions. It is a secret that has been there since the beginning of the world, "kept secret for centuries and generations past," which is now revealed among us, the author of this letter emphasizes. What is this "secret" that had been kept secret all this time and which is now revealed to us? There is an important passage here that is often missed or blurred over in many English translations. In the Greek, the key passage calling our attention is this: *ho estin christos en hymin*, rendered word for word, "which is Christ in you." If we look at the context of this, the author of the Letter to the Colossians has just given a discourse in the immediately preceding verses describing Christ as the "image of the invisible God, first born of all creation, in whom all things in heaven and on earth are created . . . by him and for him" (Col. 1:15–16), "before all things, and in whom all things consist" (1:17), "in whom all fullness dwells" (1:19). The "Christ" that is referred to and described here points us to a realm beyond linear space and time, a realm that goes beyond all of our thoughts and all of our concepts, into a realm of the infinite and vast realm of "God's power and majesty." We are ushered into a territory beyond the day-to-day world we are familiar with, pointing us to an infinite horizon beyond our ken, but a realm that nevertheless we know that we are yearning for deep within our hearts. That is the treasure that we seek; only its discovery, or recovery, can make our life complete.

And we are assured here in this passage, that this treasure is already at hand: this is the secret hidden through all the ages from generation to generation, now revealed to us openly: the secret treasure is Christ in us! We are invited to taste and see, and allow this to become a reality in us.

What do we need to do to discover, or rediscover and reclaim that treasure, the magnificent pearl, the source of joy, the source of peace, the Christ in us? This is, in one sense, a task of a lifetime. Day in, day out, it is what we are called to realize more and more fully and thoroughly every moment of our lives. But here is the good news: we are invited simply to open our eyes, here and now, and see it fully manifest before us. It is already there, given to us. Ultimately, no effort is needed, no effort on our part. It is a free gift that is given to us, right from our birth. Let us listen to that message. Those with ears, let them hear.

Reflecting on our society and culture, there are many things that come our way that somehow prevent us from appreciating what this parable conveys to us. Let us look at those things that block our way from full appreciation of that treasure, so we will be able to recognize them and put them aside or sell them or let them go. What do we need to sell off first? What do we have that prevents us from taking true possession of that which is genuinely ours? I have already mentioned a couple of factors. Is it the sense of being inadequate unless we wear this particular kind of designer clothes or shoes that everybody else is hankering for? Right from our childhood, we are hammered into this kind of mentality.

That kind of mentality feeds into us and affects our view of ourselves. The lack we may feel inside of us may drive us to aspire for some kind of authority or worldly position, to have power over others. "I desperately want to be section chief of this bureau." "I need that promotion to make me feel that I am worthy as a human being." There is always that inner sense of competition with others. If I do not get what I want, then I feel down, or I feel that I have been ignored or belittled, and I begin to resent others, especially those who have or get what I wanted but was not able to have. It can cause an identity crisis or a midlife crisis in us.

These things have been ingrained as part of our nature growing up in society where there are other individuals with whom we are called to live in community. Our little ego is always threatened by the fact that there are others out there seeking and wanting the same things I do. Jean-Paul Sartre famously said, "Hell is other people."

With that kind of mentality, we lose sight of that precious treasure that is inherent in us, and we see ourselves only in comparison with others who may have a better position or who can find a more authoritative role. And toward those who don't, we feel an air of superiority. Another gauge that we use on ourselves for our sense of identity would be the numerical figure, the amount we get for our work. Unless we get a certain amount that society looks up to as belonging to a certain successful group, we feel that we have not yet made it. These are attitudes that keep us feeling insecure as we go through the various stages of our life. Those things keep us in a situation of unease and prevent us from living at peace within ourselves.

Let us see through these things and just ask ourselves, What am I living for? For some of us, having been soaked through and through with this value system, something hits us in our forties or fifties, or even sixties, or when we are close to retirement, and we ask ourselves, What was that all about? All of the sudden we get into a very vulnerable situation. What has my life been all this time?

When we start asking such questions, we now are at a time and place in our lives where we are disposed in our mind and heart to set aside all that is unnecessary and give ourselves fully to that search for that pearl of great price, that "one thing necessary" that Jesus spoke about. What is that one thing necessary in life? For some of us who are able to find ourselves early on, that is really a tremendous blessing, that we do not have to go through a lot of twists and turns later on in life that would make life more of a struggle than it need be.

For some of us, perhaps as early as when we were in our teens or early twenties, the big questions already came to occupy our minds. Some of us are philosophically oriented from birth or through our upbringing. Some are a little more sensitive to our mortality or the fragility of human existence, because of some event that brought this home to us. Perhaps we have gone through some childhood trauma, or some painful experience, something that dislocated us early on in life, which may have been felt as tragedy or misfortune, like an illness, or the loss of a loved one or a dear friend. When we look at these events from a wider angle from the perspective of our journey of life, they may be seen rather as blessings that have enabled us to see the truth of impermanence.

Zen Master Dogen lost his mother at five and his father a few years later. That sense of dislocation, having lost those two precious caregivers in his life, predisposed him to seek the Way. He entered the monastic life at the early age of thirteen, propelled by that search for something his heart was longing for beyond all the impermanence that he was made sensitive to by the loss of both parents. Shakyamuni lost his mother right after birth, and he was cared for by his aunt. Sri Ramana Maharshi, a well-known Indian sage of the twentieth century, became morbidly preoccupied with death at the age of sixteen, and launched into a process of self-inquiry that enabled him to see through this mask of mortality that surrounds our earthly existence, and experience that which is beyond death, beyond birth and death in fact, realizing deep inner peace for the rest of his life. It is this deep inner peace that radiated from his own life that he conveyed to others who sought his teaching.

If we look at the lives of those who stand out in human history as the people about whom we can say, "I want to live like that," those individuals whom we can truly call "a gift to all humanity," just knowing that such a person exists makes us also grateful and joyful to be human. When we look at the lives of those persons, we may note how they themselves had to struggle with the fact of impermanence and mortality, and were able to see through that, thereby enabling them to realize the infinite treasure that all of us are also invited to realize, to open our eyes and see for ourselves.

With that in the background then, we might be able to understand and appreciate better the kinds of things in our lives that we may have regarded as misfortunes or tragedies. As they happened, we may have exclaimed, "Why did this have to happen to me?" Looking at them at a later phase of our lives, we might see them as the events that enabled us to seek answers to certain questions that we would not have had an occasion to seek had it not been for the misfortune or tragedy or accident.

Think of your own journey. Think of those times that you might be able to reclaim in your life and see with new eyes. In looking back, you may now be grateful for them, rather than wish that they had not happened. We are invited to look at these things and take stock of them in our own warehouse of the past, and sort them out and see which are the ones that help us in that rediscovery of that treasure of ours, and which ones we need to be cast aside, attitudes and values that simply sidetrack us from that rediscovery.

Another kind of attitude that we need to let go is one whereby one says, "If I am not doing something, I feel empty, or inadequate." It could be somebody who was a workaholic at the office; it could somebody who was a workaholic at home or a busybody who was always trying to help others and then that person might come out as a generous helper but from another angle, that person is only helping because of the need to be needed. Those are things that may be in us that prevent us from just being still and letting that infinite treasure be more fully manifest. If we notice some of those tendencies in ourselves, then we are able to take stock of them and say, what am I doing this for anyway? Maybe it will be time to give us a break and go off on a weekend retreat and examine those kinds of things going on in us, and thereby be able to set them aside and free ourselves of their influence.

Identifying our "doing" with what or who we are, our "being," is one of the pitfalls of our mode of life in this hectic workaholic society. If we define ourselves by what we do, we realize we can never do enough. We always try to prove ourselves and stake our claim to existence by doing what we think needs to be done, and yet there is never a lack of what we need to do. There is always something more, and if we cannot do more, then we have a sense of inadequacy, of frustration.

In a Zen retreat, we are invited to turn this all around and experience how our "doing" flows from a fullness of our "being." This is what the "Zen chores" are meant to invite us to experience.

Let me address this question of Zen chores. This is a part of the schedule of a Zen retreat in which we experience a way of doing that simply flows out from be-ing. As we know, the key point of a Zen retreat can be summed up in the slogan, "Don't just do something, sit there!" In short, we enter a Zen retreat to give ourselves the precious opportunity precisely to do nothing. During those three or four or seven or eight or more days we devote to a Zen retreat, we allow ourselves to simply be in silence, experiencing that be-ing, told to simply pay attention to what happens from moment to moment. And the most immediate thing that we become aware of is the fact of breathing in and breathing out.

The basic mode we take in a Zen retreat is sitting still, really doing nothing, just sitting facing the wall, breathing in and breathing out in silence, paying attention. That is the most conducive locus for us to awaken to that infinite treasure that we are. Sitting there in silence, doing nothing but breathing in and breathing out, paying attention to each moment, the dust that has accumulated in our minds may gradually fall off, and our eyes may be opened to a wondrously new horizon. This is the wondrous fact, the miracle, of *just being here, breathing in and breathing out*. This may be accompanied by the wondrous discovery that there is air that I can breathe freely, containing the oxygen that my body needs to continue being alive, that there is a ground under my feet that supports me every time I take a step, that there is water available that I can drink when I get thirsty, that there is a sky, that there are trees, that there are mountains and rivers, that there is a great wide earth containing all these wondrous things, sentient and nonsentient. Voilà, I am alive! I AM!

As our eyes are opened to that wondrous fact, we cannot help but exclaim, as Peter did when he saw Jesus transfigured in glory, "*It is good for us to be here.*" He knew he was in the presence of the Holy. That sense that ushers forth from within us—that it is *good, infinitely good* just to be here in an unconditioned way—is what we can also experience in those moments of stillness. That kind of experience can affirm us in a way that we will be set for life, in a way that nobody can take away from us. It is good for us to be here, no matter what. When we say "here," it is not a particular place as opposed to another particular place, but it is just here in an unconditioned here, wherever you are.

In a Zen retreat, we are invited to take each moment and experience it fully just as it is. It is usual to sit for six or seven, in some rigorous retreats, nine or ten hours a day in given twenty-five minute or forty-minute intervals (depending on the particular Zen lineage), interspersed by short periods of walking meditation. Besides the sitting and the walking meditation, we take our meals, do our Zen chores, and are also given times of free movement in silence, spent walking around the premises, or exercising, or relaxing. Throughout all this, one may experience what led Peter to exclaim: "It is good for us to be here!" We can taste this in the ordinary events of walking, eating together in silence, doing our assigned chores in silence, and simply relaxing.

The Zen chores are a conducive way of experiencing our be-ing that flows into doing something particular. It could be in holding a sponge in one hand and a dish with the other when washing dishes. It could be in feeling the warmth of the water on your hands. It could be in sweeping the floor. It could be in just sitting in a relaxed way while waiting for the next scheduled sit. Throughout all this, we are invited to taste that pure and exquisite experience of be-ing in the midst of whatever activity we may be engaged in. And just one glimpse of that dimension that makes us exclaim "It is good for us to be here!" can give us the firm assurance for the rest of our lives, that we are in the presence of the Holy, that everything we do is immersed in that infinite horizon that is our true home.

This is an invitation to let whatever we do be an outflow from that unconditioned affirmation of our being. As we do so, we are able to find that whatever we do is no longer driven by an inner need to be busy so that I can "feel worthy." Precisely as what I do comes as an outflow of my being, I experience whatever I do now as my gift to the universe, with whatever outcome it may have.

With this way of seeing, we are given the freedom to discern which things we do are more important than others. This way of giving ourselves as a gift to the universe by what we do enables us to prioritize and select what those things are that we can do as an outflow of our being, and thus do things not out of compulsions or necessity, but out of the sheer freedom of giving ourselves as a gift.

Now I would like to offer a passage written by someone who awakened to that treasure in his own life, and consider how it shed light on the rest of his life from that point on. Here is a passage from the writings of Thomas Merton which appears in his journals, but also excerpted in a book called *Conjectures of a Guilty Bystander*. This is the account of an experience he had in the middle of the city of Louisville when he was out doing errands, while standing on at the corner of Fourth and Walnut. This is one example of a person who, in some unexpected way, was just walking down the street when he suddenly realizes that treasure in the field we were talking about.

In Louisville, at the corner of Fourth and Walnut, in the center of the shopping district, I was suddenly overwhelmed with the realization that I loved all those people, and that they were mine, and I theirs, that we could not be alien to one another, not even though we were total strangers. It was like waking from a dream of separateness, of furious self-isolation. . . .

. . . This sense of liberation from an illusory difference was such a relief and such a joy to me that I almost laughed out loud, and I suppose my happiness could have taken form in the words, thank God, thank God that I am like the other people there, that I am only a human being among all others.

. . . I have the immense joy of being human, a member of a race in which God himself became incarnate. As to the sorrow and stupidities of the human condition that overwhelm me, now I realize what we all are. And if only everybody could realize this, but it cannot be explained. There is no way of telling people that they are all walking around shining like the sun.

. . . There are no strangers. Then it was as if I suddenly saw the secret beauty of their hearts, the depths of their hearts where neither sin, nor desire nor self-knowledge can reach, the core of their reality, the person that each one is in God's eyes. If only they could all see themselves as they really are. If only we could see each other that way all the time, there would be no more war, no more hatred, no more cruelty, and no more greed. I suppose the big problem would be that we would fall down and worship each other, but this cannot be seen, only believed and understood by a peculiar gift. . .

. . . It is in everybody, and if we could see it, we could see these billions of points of light coming together, in the face and blaze of a sun that would make all the darkness and cruelty of life vanish completely. I have no program for this seeing. It is only given, but the gate of heaven is everywhere. It is only given. . . . I have no program for this seeing.

In this passage, Thomas Merton realizes something that freed him from that ego-delusion that puts a veil on our eyes and prevents us from seeing the true nature of things, that prevents us from beholding the glory that is always there.

That glimpse enabled him to see all of those people walking in front of him, and by extension, each and every one born into this world, as an intimate part and parcel of himself. There is an unveiling that happens here, whereby he is able to see through this wall that separates us from one another.

That glimpse that enabled him to exclaim that "they were mine, and I theirs" empowered him to become a voice for the sentiments of the people of his time, to feel their pains and struggles as his own.

That glimpse that we too can be opened to bring us out of this shell of ego-delusion, can open us to realize what or who we truly are. We are invited to continue to cultivate that stillness so that one little opening might give us that whole scenario, whereby we see, and bodily realize, that we are one, we are connected, and we are together.

The treasure in the field is not some kind of jewel that we can objectify as out there. For those of us who may be practicing with a koan, we might be misled into thinking that there is something in there that we need to know or learn about or grasp. It is like my imagining that Helen would be in the baggage claim area and looking where she was not. Let us let go of all of our preconceptions and simply listen to what is. With every breath, just take that breath. When the bird chirps, just let the bird chirp. When we hear the rustle of the wind through the leaves, just let that be. Let that be, and, if I may use some words that might be misleading, *be that*. When I say be that, the analogy is faulty because it is an imperative, but there is no need to be imperative about it. You are that, and you will understand, if you are disposed to listening truly. That is why the parables are always accompanied by the invitation, "Those who have ears, let them hear. Those who have eyes, let them see." What we are engaged in, this enterprise of sitting in stillness, is one that entails clearing the dust from our eyes, clearing the blockage from our ears, so that we can truly see and hear in a way that everything becomes transparent. You are the treasure in the field and the pearl of great price.

Merton notes in the passage above that he has no "program" for this seeing, as he acknowledges it to be a pure gift of grace. Yet his own life, beginning with his search for truth as described in his *Seven-Storey Mountain*, continuing with his entry into the monastic life, was his way of disposing himself to receive this pure gift. It is not a "program," but an open heart and mind, willing to give oneself fully, whatever it takes, so that the treasure may come into one's life. His entry into the monastic life, and his total obedience to whatever that entailed, was his way of "selling everything" for the sake of the treasure. Each one of us is required to do nothing less: a willingness to give one's all for the sake of the treasure of our True Self. This is what Zen practice invites us to give: nothing less than our whole dedication to the practice and fullness of attention in each present moment.

Zen offers a structured way of helping us set aside the obstructions that prevent us from seeing our True Face. Let us take the invitation that the Zen tradition offers to us, to sit and be still, taking its prescriptions for a posture conducive to stillness, paying attention with each breath, and allowing the mind to be fully there in each present moment. This is what "just sitting" is about. This is what we may call "a program that is no program." So let us take that, and be open to what happens along the way.

Chapter Four

▷─┼─◈〉──◎──〈◈─┼─◁

Blessed Are You
(Matthew 5:1–3, 8–9)

*When Jesus saw the crowds, he went up the mountain; and
after he sat down, his disciples came to him. Then he began to
speak, and taught them, saying:*

*Blessed are the poor in spirit, for theirs is the kingdom of
heaven . . .*

Blessed are the pure in heart, for they will see God.

—Matthew 5:1–3, 8–9

Blessed

This theme of "blessed" runs through the nine proclamations called the Beatitudes, found in Matthew 5:3–11, with another version in Luke 6:20–22. Another English word used to translate the Greek word *makarioi* is "happy."

We may tend to read these passages thinking that what follows the word "blessed," that is, "poor in spirit," "meek," "those who mourn" and so forth, are conditions for receiving the blessing, or for realizing the state of being blessed. However, if we look closely, it will be clear that these passages are not about conditions at all. It is not "*If* you are this or that (poor in spirit, meek, etc.), *then* you are, or will be, blessed." Or "*If* you become poor in spirit, then you will enter the kingdom of heaven," and so on. Rather, these statements simply affirm a fact that those who are poor in spirit, meek, peacemakers, and so on, are blessed, *just as they are.* What is the message for us here?

Let us first look at this initial word "blessed" that runs throughout the nine items called the Beatitudes. The Israelites, as they are described in their own scriptures, understood themselves to be a people chosen especially by the Holy One, the Creator of the universe, for a specific purpose on this earth. They referred to this Holy One by a tetragram, YHWH, which they did not dare pronounce due to their exceeding deference to the holiness and power of that to which the term referred, and instead they used the word *Adonai* (Lord). Most English translations render this term "God," so we will also follow this usage.

They understood that God spoke to them directly through specially chosen individuals, the prophets. They were a people set apart, chosen to proclaim God's glory to the nations, and to announce God's promise to all of creation.

The opening book of the Holy Scriptures of the Jewish tradition, the book of Genesis, begins with the story of the creation of the universe. It is the story of how God brings forth the elements one by one, the firmament, the sea, the mountains, the plants and animals, and finally, human beings. Looking over what has now been brought forth, "*God saw that it was good, that it was very good.*" God's proclamation that all of creation is very good means that each and every thing in creation has received God's blessing, as participating in the very goodness of God.

Each and every thing in this universe has been given that affirmation: *God saw that it was good.* The sky, the earth, the oceans, the mountains—all these are good, just as they are. Each and every one of us is good, just as we are. This is the first message we are invited to hear as we sit there breathing in and breathing out. Listen to that primal word from the depths of our being, proclaiming: *You are good.* We have not earned this goodness; we have done nothing to merit it. It is simply what we are, what we have been right from the very start.

We did not work for it. We are already that, right from the core of our being, right in the place where we acknowledge and recognize ourselves to be. When we acknowledge ourselves as *just here, just now* we receive that cosmic and unconditional affirmation: *You are good, just as you are!* This is the first point in understanding what the word "blessed" means for us.

You are blessed. This is our first hint, namely that we simply need to listen and allow that original blessing to become palpable, clearer to us, and more immediate, because it never leaves us. It is never separated from us. We are always blessed.

One element from our upbringing in a Christian tradition that may need to be clarified is the notion of "original sin." It may have been conveyed to us in a way that made us think that sin is inherent in our nature as human beings. Western Christianity in particular has been heavily influenced by the teachings of Saint Augustine on fallen humanity, bolstered further by Martin Luther and the reformer's writings on the depravity of the human condition bereft of grace.

As we reflectively read the scriptural accounts (Gen. 1–3) that are taken as the background of this teaching, we can see how it is grossly misleading to attach the qualifier "original" to the word "sin." What is truly "original," that with which the entire created universe is endowed with right from the start, is the blessing coming from the unconditional affirmation, "*God saw that it was good.*" The "sin" of disobedience committed by Adam and Eve is not at all an "original" feature of our human condition, but rather an outcome of a human refusal to accept the divine offer.[1]

This divine blessing constitutes our original nature. It is given to us, and to all of creation, right from the start. *You are blessed.* The mountains, the rivers, the sun, the moon, the stars—everything that lives and breathes on this earth—all are blessed.

Sin entered the scene when we human beings started behaving in ways that forgot the original blessing or took it for granted. We have distorted our understanding of ourselves as originally blessed, and we have separated ourselves from that source of blessing by our pride and self-delusions. Now it is time to acknowledge that distortion and delusion, and come back to where we have been right from the start.

We may have been led to believe, through a misguided religious upbringing, that we are worthless because of an inherently sinful nature. Or we may have come under the influence of the society and culture around us relaying all sorts of distorted messages, telling us that we can be worthy only if we have acquired this or that particular material possession or have reached a certain achievement based on our own efforts. We are now invited to see through these distorted views and assume a wholesome, and rightful, view of ourselves.

Our original state is a state of unconditional blessing. We are given this state of blessing gratuitously and freely. We did not merit it; we did not ask for it; we did not, and we cannot, work for it. We need simply be humble enough to acknowledge the fact: *You are blessed.* This blessing is ours right from the start. We need not exert any additional effort to attain it.

---

[1] This was also called to our attention in recent times by Matthew Fox, in his book *Original Blessing* (New York: Putnam, 2000).

Really, there is nothing to attain; it has already been given. If anything, we have separated ourselves from this blessing for reasons that I have already noted, but also perhaps because of some sense of false pride. We imagine that we must prove ourselves and that we have to merit God's blessing. We mistakenly believe that we must "do good" and try to achieve something, and then we will feel comfortable accepting God's blessing, as if we have earned it. This is a false pride that prevents us from accepting that we are blessed. This is a theme to which we will continue to return.

Just take a moment, sit there and immerse yourself in what that message conveys. *You are blessed, just as you are.* Don't get it wrong: we do not take on this spiritual practice of sitting in meditation as a "means" of attaining this blessed state. We do not venture off on retreats in order to be worthy of receiving God's blessing. No, we attend retreats to give ourselves the opportunity to sit in stillness, give ourselves the leeway to open the eyes and ears of our heart, and thereby realize our blessed state given to us even before we sought it.

The practices we undertake during a Zen retreat, centered on sitting still and listening in silence, and all the other elements included as prescriptions for paying attention to each breath and in each moment, are not "meritorious acts" that we practice so that we might be worthy of receiving something like enlightenment or whatever fruits this practice might bring about in our lives. They can be considered simply as ways by which we set aside whatever obstructs our view and prevents us from realizing what is already given to us right from the start.

What are those obstacles? They are our delusions, self-pride, and mistaken sense of self-worth based on what we may have attained or accomplished for ourselves. We may go on in our life mistakenly thinking that it is all about piling up achievements, from the grades we receive in school, to the merit badges we accumulate in the various kinds of activities we are driven to by our parents or peers, to the amount we may get in our paycheck, the number of friends we can count on Facebook, and so on. In going through these hoops we face in the various stages of our human life, we think we are making something of ourselves as we achieve some kind of success in them. Or conversely, we may have judged ourselves a failure because we were not able to attain those things that others seem to have attained, or we have not been able to possess those things that everybody else thinks are necessary to be happy in this life. Either way, whether we consider ourselves "successful," based on our supposed attainments, or a "failure," based on not having attained those things, such a life runs on a fundamental delusion. This is the delusion of a separate ego-consciousness that I identify with myself.

Sitting still and paying attention to each breath from moment to moment enables us to clear the way and to be able to see through these deluded views. Let me offer some more practical pointers here. If you are struggling during your sitting because distractions continually creep up on you, like thoughts about home or your personal issues, the recommendation here is just to recognize those thoughts, let them be, breathe them out with the outbreath, and continue sitting. Just keep coming back to the breath. Breathe in and breathe out. Let yourself be, and realize that it is all right, even with those struggles and issues we all face in our concrete human existence. We are accepted just as we are, in and through our own struggles, in and through our failures, as well as whatever we may consider our successes. These are aspects of the blessing that we are.

We are familiar with the phrase, "a blessing in disguise." This is the kind of blessing that we are not readily able to recognize as such when it comes into our lives, that is, as a blessing.

If we are of a certain age, we surely would have had our share of pain, suffering, disappointment, betrayal, or some kind of tragedy in our lives. When they happened to us, most likely we took them as something that threw us off our paths or hit us in a painful way that we thought we were incapable of bearing. In those moments, we may have shouted to the heavens, "Why does this have to happen to me?" As we were going through that painful experience or suffering or struggle in our lives, we may been preoccupied with our little egos that were hurt in the process and may not have been able to see that experience or event in all that it contained for us.

I would like to invite each one of you to just take a look at that whole panorama of your life, from the time you were born, growing up, going through all the different things you have gone through, and all the way up to this moment. It can be very salutary to take time to give ourselves this opportunity to reexamine our own personal history. As we do this, we may be able to see those particular scenes from new angles and in the context of the total scenario. As we examine especially those events that were painful, those that we may still wish we had never had to bear in the first place, we may be able to recognize the glimmer of a silver lining in them. My suggestion here is to look again with new eyes on those moments that we may have considered our "dark nights."

To clarify, I am not saying here that in the face of a great tragedy such as the loss of a loved one, that we should consider that a blessing. That would be an outright lie, even a blasphemy, to think in that way. A tragedy is a tragedy; a painful experience is a painful experience that can never be assuaged with pious words.

What I am suggesting here, however, is something from a different angle. Is it possible that, in that time of grief, perhaps an important message was being conveyed to us, but we were too preoccupied with grief to be able to recognize or appreciate it? I invite us to imagine that we might be able to see things in a different way.

This is an invitation. If we have some issues that we need to work out in our lives, some issues of unresolved pain, grief, or trauma, a retreat may be a conducive time to be able to review them and consider them in a new light. I do not recommend this to be done during times of formal sitting meditation. During those times of formal sitting, what I recommend is to simply sit in as stable a position as your bodily constitution allows, and breathe in and breathe out, and again, breathe in and breathe out, paying attention to each breath. For some who have been in the practice of sitting for some time now, you may have been given some general guidelines like repeating a sacred word or just sitting following the breath and coming back to the breath each time.

As you notice your mind wandering, just come back to the breath each time. And as you do, bring your mind again to the here and now with each breath. Allow it to remain in that stillness. In that stillness you may hear a message from deep within, addressing you. *You are blessed.* You are good, infinitely good, and absolutely good. Just sit and be, and let that word of blessing resound throughout your entire being, and bring you to deep, deep inner peace.

You may ask yourself, how can this be? We all have our own particular issues we are still struggling with. We may have lost someone dear to us, or we may be struggling with some difficult challenges. Perhaps our finances are in a mess, and we do not know how we will make it through the next couple of weeks. Realizing all of this, how can we say that we are blessed? That can be considered a koan that we are invited to look at straight in the eye. A koan is a challenge that, on its surface, seems to be an insoluble contradiction. How can I be truly *blessed* when there are still so many issues unresolved in my life, when there is still so much I need to reckon with? This is the koan stated plain and simple, which each of us may be able to identify with. Zen invites us to simply sit with this, and "be one" with it. Be still, and know.

Brother David Steindl-Rast, a well-known spiritual guide and writer, comes to mind here, for an important message he conveys in many of his talks and writings. One of the key themes in his talks and writings is that of gratefulness.[2] That is the natural and spontaneous response that wells up in our hearts as we come to hear, and realize, this fact: *You are blessed.*

As we receive this original blessing and truly acknowledge it and realize that it is I who is being addressed here, there is nothing I can do but accept it in all humility, with a heart full of gratitude. This gratitude will naturally well up and flow into thoughts, words, and actions, which will transform our lives. From that point on, when we are able to acknowledge that blessedness, then we will live our lives in a manner that no longer seeks advantage over another or seeks to search for our own gain or our own success. Our lives will no longer be lives of grasping or seeking to compare ourselves with others, fighting for our own security. Instead, our lives will be a way of expressing gratitude for that blessedness that we are. How are we to express that gratitude? Again, each one of us is called to live out our given blessing. When we recognize that it is a blessing given freely to us, the concrete thoughts, words, and acts of gratitude that result will mark how we live the rest of our lives.

I conclude this section noting two movements that occur as we sit in stillness. The first is the movement of receiving, acknowledging, accepting, absorbing. Our whole being comes to be immersed in that affirmation: *You are blessed.* With every step, with every breath, with every sound, with every color,

---

[2] David Steindl-Rast, *Gratefulness, the Heart of Prayer: An Approach to Life in Fullness* (Mahwah, NJ: Paulist Press, 1984).

with every taste of food, with each and every thing that we experience throughout the day, we receive 10,000 blessings, 1,000,000 blessings. Each moment is filled with blessings. As we experience each moment as a blessing, each tree as a blessing, each sound as a blessing, gratitude will well up from within our hearts. This is the second movement. The way we live from this moment on is simply an expression of gratitude, gratitude, gratitude, gratitude. We will take our meal as an act of gratitude. We look at a tree with a look of gratitude. We look at the persons around us, hearts welling forth with gratitude. Simply gratitude for the fact that each and every one of us is right here, gratitude that the world is there, in spite of or even in the midst of its pains and sorrows. This is another koan we can look at straight in the eye.

If each and every one of us can live our lives simply acknowledging and appreciating that blessing, and living in gratitude as an outflow of that blessing, then how different a world this would be. Let us start right here, where each and every one of us is simply living in a manner that acknowledges that blessing and letting it flow out into gratitude in thought, word, and action. With each breath, let that sink in, and let us taste that with our whole being. Let us be immersed in that, and our hearts will be filled for a lifetime.

Blessed Are the Poor in Spirit

Blessed are the poor in spirit, for theirs is the kingdom of heaven.

Many of us spend a great part of our lives trying to find out who we are, trying to find our place in the world. As we acknowledge ourselves to be in this search, the opening statement in the series of the nine Beatitudes may have an important message for us.

What does this phrase entail? What is it saying to us? First of all, we must note a difference in terminology between the Gospel of Matthew, which says "Blessed are the poor in spirit," and the Gospel of Luke, which says simply, "Blessed are the poor." Different biblical commentators address the different nuances of these two expressions. In looking at the context of Luke's Gospel, we see "the poor" as the marginalized in society, those who are bereft of such basic necessities as food, shelter, and clothing. Luke is saying outright, "Blessed are the poor."

Recall that Luke is the same writer of the Good News who also gave us the powerful prayer and song of Mary, widely known as the *Magnificat* ("My soul magnifies the Lord"). This song comes spontaneously from Mary's heart when she meets her cousin Elizabeth, who recognizes that she is bearing the Holy One in her flesh. Mary proclaims, "The Mighty One has brought down the powerful from their thrones, and has lifted the lowly . . . has filled the hungry with good things, and has sent the rich away empty." These "lowly" and "hungry" are the same ones Luke refers to when he writes, "Blessed are the poor." Luke also pays special attention to the widow, the orphan, and the stranger. Another well-known gospel passage in Luke that is not found in the other gospels is the story of the Good Samaritan, the traveler from the region of Samaria, whose people were disdained and looked down upon, discriminated against by the mainstream Jewish society at the time. It is the Samaritan, in contrast to the temple priest and the legal expert who ignore and bypass a man lying wounded along the way, who steps down from his donkey and takes care of this wounded one. Jesus upholds him as closest to the reign of God, as the one who fulfills God's will on earth. Through all these narratives, Luke's message can be read in this way: those who are regarded as the lowly ones in society and set aside by others are the ones preferred by and closer to the heart of God.

The Gospel of Matthew adds the qualifier "in spirit": "Blessed are the poor in spirit." No matter what one's position in society may be, no matter what one's actual economic status or political alignment, the "poor in spirit" receive God's favor. Who then are "the poor in spirit"?

I recall some incidents that happened to persons I know, that convey to me a glimpse of what it means to be "poor in spirit."

I was part of a group that conducted what are called "immersion trips," visits by small groups from Japan to my own country, the Philippines, for the purpose of mutual understanding, solidarity, and cooperation between people of these two countries. Some groups included students of the university where I was teaching, and others were organized by Catholic communities and included laypersons, priests, and Catholic nuns. The visitors from Japan would be assigned to live with families in a poor urban area or a rural farming area in the Philippines, to experience life as lived by the people in those localities. After the period of immersion in the lives of the families to which they were assigned, the visitors would then come together to reflect on share what they had learned, with a view to understanding better how they could work hand in hand with the people whom they met in their visits, across geographical distances and national boundaries, toward a more humane, more just, and equitable society for all.

A Catholic sister who happened to join in on one of the immersion trips brought back a story for us. She was assigned to live with a family that consisted of a couple and their seven children. The father was a laborer in a factory, and the mother earned money by doing laundry and house cleaning for other families in the vicinity. The sister related how she was at an evening meal with the family. The children of various ages were all gathered around the table, and they all had their empty plate before them. The rice was first passed around, and there was barely enough for each one, the father and the mother taking the smallest share. Then a platter was brought to the table with two fish. Of course, being the guest, the sister was offered the platter, and after saying thanks, she graciously took one of the fish and put it on her plate, assuming that there would be more fish coming for the others. After the grace before meal was said, the signal to eat was given, and so she started to help herself to the fish. She had had a long day, visiting the factories which employed many of the people who lived in the area, talking to youth and people from all walks of life, listening to explanations about their economic and social and religious situation, and so on. So she was tired and ready to enjoy a good meal with her host family. She continued eating, and then as she looked around, to her shock, she realized that the other fish of the two that were on the platter was all that was left for the rest of the family, seven children and the father and mother as well. But it was too late for her to do anything at that point, having already consumed much of the fish she had on her plate. She then observed how everyone was in good spirits, smiling as each one took a bit of the remaining fish as it was passed around, and ate it with their rice to their heart's content. They were all smiling and talking about different things in their language that the sister could not understand, but she could tell that they were having a good time nevertheless, especially inspired and gladdened by the fact that they had a guest from Japan taking a meal with them. Every now and then during the meal the father or the mother would turn to her, and ask her in English, is the food okay? Are you enjoying your meal? To this she could only reply with an embarrassed smile, nodding her head to say yes, trying her best not to reveal the difficult emotions she was struggling with during that time. When she went back to her room she

could not help the tears that welled up, with all the complicated sentiments that went with them.

This reminds me of another story related by a young
woman from Europe, whom we will call Maria, who came
to stay with a family in a poor area in Manila for a week.
The host was a widow who had three daughters. The widow
earned a livelihood by washing clothes and doing whatever
odd jobs she could find. Her daughters helped out by going
out and vending various items or by working part-time at a
retail store in the area. This widow, named Rosita, had taken in
a small boy of about five years old from a neighboring family
who had a history of violence, and was rearing him as part of
her own family, even though she already had three children.
One afternoon, Maria came back from some errands with
a box of ice cream for the family. She took the box of ice
cream from her bag and showed it to Rosita and her children,
who were delighted and eager to receive it and partake of it
together. But the very first thing that Rosita did after receiving the ice cream was to ask one of her daughters to bring
some plastic containers from the kitchen. Then Rosita took
portions of the ice cream and put them in these containers,
and instructed her daughters, "Bring this to the neighbor to
the right, and this one to so and so, and that one to the other
family over there." There was just enough left for her children
to have a helping each, so as the daughters came back from the
neighbors with the empty containers, they all partook of the
ice cream together with gladness and joy, thankful to Maria
for having brought it.

The two incidents convey a picture of two different families who had their own share of the struggles of life, who
may not have had all they could have wanted in material possessions or opportunities for social mobility, and so on, but
who showed a magnanimity of heart, the kind that gives us a

glimpse of what Matthew must have meant when he wrote in his gospel, "Blessed are the poor in spirit."

I offer another true story in this vein. The news of the gigantic tsunami that swept over large areas in Asia, taking the lives of over 250,000 people in Indonesia, India, Sri Lanka, Thailand, and other countries, shook people all over the world, and still reverberates in our collective memory. In the midst of that big tragedy, it was heartwarming that people all over the world responded with generosity, taking up collections to send to those areas affected to help in the relief efforts. A young daughter of a close family friend, whom we shall call Claire, was in middle school at the time, and when she heard the news about the tsunami and learned of the collections being taken up, without batting an eye she took out her entire savings, from several years of birthday and Christmas gifts, which at that time amounted to $486, and sent it in with all the donations for the tsunami victims. *Blessed are the poor in spirit.*

There are so many other angles we can consider to better understand and appreciate the gospel message, "Blessed are the poor in spirit," and how it is presented in Hebrew scriptures as well as in the New Testament. This is the spirit that Jesus himself embodied, which he also taught his disciples to cultivate.

> *Do not store up for yourselves treasures on earth, where moth and rust destroy, and where thieves break in and steal. But store up for yourselves treasures in heaven, where neither moth nor rust destroys, and where thieves do not break in or steal; for where your treasure is, there your heart will be also. (Matt. 6:19–21)*

This is an attitude of heart and mind that is also called evangelical poverty. This mode of being is not preoccupied with one's own self-aggrandizement at the expense of others, or of bolstering up one's power and one's possessions, but has a heart and mind totally open to be of service to others. It is the same spirit of total openness and transparency that Mary, mother of Jesus, manifested in her own life, up to the end, as she stood by her son at the foot of the Cross. It is the spirit also manifested by Jesus' followers, as we learn about how they gathered together in community in the Acts of the Apostles.

> *And all those who had believed were together and had all things in common; and they began selling their property and possessions and were sharing them with all, as anyone might have need. Day by day continuing with one mind in the temple, and breaking bread from house to house, they were taking their meals together with gladness and sincerity of heart. (Acts 2:44–46)*

And further,

> *There were no needy persons among them. For from time to time those who owned land or houses sold them, brought the money from the sales and put it at the apostles' feet, and it was distributed to anyone who had need. (Acts 4:34–35)*

Since the early centuries, the spirit of nonattachment to the things of this world was a key feature of Christian spirituality. This is the spirit of those who take the vow of poverty, freeing themselves to be entirely at the service of proclaiming the Good News to others, following Jesus' invitation.

> *If you want to be perfect, go, sell your possessions and give to the poor, and you will have treasure in heaven. Then come, follow me. (Matt. 19:21)*

It is a vow to free oneself from the need to look for, seek, or work for possessions for one's own self, a vow that one will divest one's self of any of such wishes and any such holdings and simply depend on what one is given by others. This is the same spirit of poverty embodied by those in the Buddhist tradition who, following the example of Shakyamuni Buddha, forsake worldly ambition, set aside their worldly possessions, and give their lives wholly to the path of awakening, joining a monastic community for this end. Because of that freedom, one is able to give oneself to the dharma wholeheartedly, and likewise serve the people in the best possible way, without being hindered by the quest for possessions or by worldly attachments.

Institutionally, though, there is an irony here that those who have taken this vow of poverty have the privilege of being able to live in the most comfortable places. When I was still a Jesuit, I would visit the United States from Japan. The Jesuit house I would stay in while in New York is the Jesuit Residence on East 83rd Street. It is a saying by people around the area that "the only ones who could afford to live there are either millionaires or those who have a vow of poverty." This is not to demean or criticize the Jesuits who live there as their base for their work in the service of others, nor to say that they should not have a house in that area. That is just one of those ironies of institutional religious life that the individuals who are part of the institution need to continue to take stock of and work with, to maintain fidelity to the spirit that brought about the institution in the first place.

What I am describing here is the invitation that the gospels present to each and every one of us. How can we live in a way of total freedom from seeking material and even spiritual goods, in a way that allows us to be free and enables us to offer our lives for the service of others? I would like to offer a Zen koan that might give us a hint in that regard.

This is a koan from a collection called the Mumonkan, or Gateless Gate, that addresses this question of what "poor in spirit" is all about, in a way that can open us to a new dimension for appreciating the first Beatitude.

> *A monk, Seizei, eagerly asks Master Sosan, "I am alone and poor. I beg you Master, please help me become prosperous."*
>
> *Sosan said, "Venerable Zei!"*
>
> *"Yes Master," replied Seizei.*
>
> *Sosan said, "See, you have already drunk three cups of fine wine and still you say that you have not yet moistened your lips."*

That is the koan. What is this all about? The commentary from the thirteenth-century Zen monk Wumen (Mumon), gives us a hint in taking what the monk Seizei may have meant: *Seizei is obsequious in tone, but what is his real intention?*

Mumon is suggesting that Seizei is not really being upfront or straightforward in calling himself "poor." "I am poor; please help me become prosperous." That is not to be taken literally. Seizei has a Zen eye here, the eye of awakening, and he may be testing Master Sosan in saying what he said. And Master Sosan, true to form, responds accordingly. Sosan likewise has a penetrating eye and thoroughly sees through the monk's state of mind. "Be that as it may, just tell me, where and how has the Venerable Zei drunk the wine."

"I am alone and poor; please help me become prosperous." The Master says in response, *"Venerable Zei!" "Yes, Master."* Seizei replies to the Master's call. *"See, you have already drunk three full cups of wine, and you still say that you are thirsty."* It is like holding the loot and still saying you are innocent. What is this about?

How is Seizei poor? And yet how is it also that he is said to be drinking cups of fine wine affordable only to the richest persons in China? Where are those cups of wine that he is supposed to be drinking? That is the koan.

The practitioners who work with this are asked to sit down and empty themselves in silence, breathing in and breathing out, to come to that point of true aloneness, true poverty, and to realize and see and drink for themselves those three cups of wine that Seizei had drunk. Wumen, the editor of this collection, adds a verse to help practitioners appreciate the irony of this koan:

Poor like Hantan,
Of a spirit like Ko
Though they cannot sustain themselves,
They compete with one another for wealth.

Hantan is a legendary figure in Chinese lore, who was, as they say, as poor as a church mouse, or in this case better to say temple mouse, a jolly person and free spirit who roamed around villages greeting and talking to people, entering taverns and winning everybody's goodwill; they competed in offering him free drinks. Ko was a legendary general who is said to have had such courage that he was able to snatch a sword from the mouth of a ravenous tiger. Seizei was a monk who owned no material possessions and held no worldly rank or social privileges. Those who have realized the mind and heart of Seizei, who have divested themselves of any claim to worldly possessions, are those with untold riches and a spirit of magnanimity, and they are unequalled in this world.

In not having any possessions themselves, owning nothing, they were free in spirit to realize that the whole universe is their own, and that there was nothing in it that is not theirs. That is the hint that we are given here. If we divest ourselves of any claim to this little part of the earth's property and become totally nothing, then literally, there is nothing that is not ours. That is the irony that we are invited to take in and realize, and see how infinitely rich we all are, once we pass through this gate of being poor in spirit.

It is like the state of mind of the Zen monk who was asked by his abbot to deliver a precious golden statue of Buddha to a neighboring temple. The Zen monk was waylaid by robbers who took not only the golden Buddha but also the cart used to transport it, and along with that, the very clothes of the monk himself. On top of that, they beat up the monk and left him unconscious by the side of the road. Coming to his senses in the middle of the night, the monk looked around, realized that the Buddha was gone, the cart gone with it, and so were his clothes. He looked up and saw the moon shining in full brilliance above, lighting up the mountain scenery in the background. At this, he said, thinking of the robbers who took the precious Buddha, "Ah, look at that. I wish I could have given them that beautiful moon as well!"

Blessed are the poor in spirit, for theirs is the kingdom of heaven.

Let us take the invitation to realize this beatitude by simply sitting, breathing in and breathing out. As we do so, take the opportunity to empty our selves of anything that we may still cling to or hold on to or aspire to or identify as our own fame. Let us simply take each breath. When we take each breath, breathing in, receive that with gratitude, stopping and tasting the silence, and breathing out, empty out everything that stands in the way of the realization of *the infinite fullness of this present moment.*

This is our key to unraveling the koan above. Both the monk Seizei and Master Sosan, who have each in their own ways realized their True Self backed by their earnest practice of Zen, are both endowed with the eye of awakening, and so are able to experience the infinite fullness of this present moment, each present moment. So in making an utterance, "I am alone and poor. Please help me become prosperous," in that very moment Seizei is experiencing this infinite fullness in the very act of saying what he was saying. And as Master Sosan responds by addressing him, "Venerable Zei!" he hears that with full attention, and in that moment, he is also experiencing this infinite fullness. One fine cup of wine on top of another. Now the reader can continue and point out where to find the third cup of wine here in this koan. But knowing how it works in the koan is an entirely different matter than experiencing that infinite fullness of the present moment for oneself. This is the invitation offered to us by the practice of sitting in stillness, breathing in, breathing out, emptying ourselves of anything our little ego-consciousness may still be holding on to.

We are invited to empty ourselves and become truly nothing, in the same way as Mary in the *Magnificat* declared her nothingness before the infinite power of the Holy One. Experientially arriving at that point of nothingness, which I like to call "zero-point," that "still point of the turning world," we stand at the fulcrum of the entire universe. That zero-point that we are invited to experience is where the whole universe is held together, where we are able to freely experience the infinite fullness and richness of everything in the universe, *just as it is.* That is our home, truly. Let us set aside all the debris that prevents us from arriving home and come to that point ourselves. The *kin-dom* of heaven is there, waiting to be realized.

But again, it is important to emphasize that it is not our efforts that will get us there. For an angle to help us understand this point better, I recall what I learned from the life of a saint we studied when I was a Jesuit novice. This is about Saint Aloysius Gonzaga, who was a Jesuit in training who died in his late twenties before he could be ordained as a priest. In his short life, he was able to embody what it means to be truly poor in spirit and yet endowed with the infinite richness of divine life. Aloysius Gonzaga came from a noble and affluent family, and was raised in an environment of luxury and wealth. He was drawn to a religious vocation in his late teens and entered the Jesuits, forsaking his worldly status and the tremendous material wealth that would have been his had he wanted it. As he was receiving formation as a Jesuit, seeking to align his entire life with the divine will so he could fully be at the service of God's people as a Jesuit, he engaged himself in the disciplines and practices of spirituality, centered on the Spiritual Exercises of Saint Ignatius of Loyola. In reflecting on his own life, he realized that his affluent background and conditioning had twisted his inner being in a way that made him susceptible to attachments and luxury. He tended to compare himself to a bent tree that needed extra effort to unbend itself and straighten itself. That was his way of explaining why he needed to exert effort in disciplining himself, not to get any extra merit through his striving or attain something that he did not yet have.

So all our effort in our spiritual practice is not geared toward attaining something we do not yet have, but it is precisely a way to straighten out the distorted way of looking at things that we have been conditioned to by our upbringing. It is not effort directed at getting something as a result, but as our cooperative response toward undoing those unwholesome habits of ours that prevent us from opening our hearts and minds and being able to hear that primal word, or to see our Original Face.

This effort takes the form of sitting still and trying to keep our minds still. This is simply our way of coming back to the pristine purity we all are when we are born and undoing all of those things that twisted us along the way so that we can be simpler and more direct and transparent in the face of that which called us out of nothingness toward the fullness of being. Listening in silence in this way is an undoing of our twisted nature in order to be more pliant and able to hear that word that tells us, *You are blessed.* That is what being poor in spirit entails, namely acknowledging that we have nothing for ourselves, nothing to offer except our own twisted nature that we need to "untwist." Like Mary, in acknowledging that we are nothing before the infinite fullness of the Holy One, we lay ourselves open to that visit of the Holy One in our own lives.

The Kin-dom in Our Midst

The first beatitude proclaims, "Blessed are the poor in spirit, for theirs is the kingdom of heaven." This phrase in English comes from the Greek expression, *basileia tou theou*, which literally means, the place where God is sovereign—the reign of God. What is this all about? And how does it resonate with what we are already experiencing as we sit in silence? Commentators point out that it is not so much a place or a realm or a domain; it can be more accurately described as a state of affairs where God's will reigns. When everything happens according to God's will, when it is God's will that reigns over all, then the messianic age is here. This means that everything we are all expecting and hoping for deep within our hearts, the coming of God in our midst, is now at hand. This is the reign of God. That is the Good News that Jesus proclaims: the reign of God is *at hand*; it is immediate; it is before us and impinging on us. Simply let it happen by opening your hearts to it. *Metanoia* means to have a change of heart, to change the direction of your heart, from one preoccupied by your little petty pursuits driven by your insecure ego-consciousness, to one that is totally open to God in trust, welcoming God into your hearts. That is Jesus' invitation to us.

The reign of God is right here before us, waiting to enter into our lives, so let us just be open to it and welcome its coming. This is the invitation being extended to us constantly. This points back to the second theme examined earlier, to be "poor in spirit," to let go of your attachments and your tendency to be driven by your insecurities that make you want to hold on to things or to grasp for power over others. Instead, just be your natural self, just be as you are without any layers of cosmetic on your face, without any pretense, without any attempt to pretend you are what you are not. *Simply acknowledge that you are nothing before the Holy One.* Recall Mary, in all her transparency and openness, who was suffused with divine grace and presence. That was the mark of her life, namely to be simply a transparent receptacle that received God's presence into her entire being, a transparent vessel that thus conveyed God's presence in the world. She bore the Child of God in her own bodily being and brought that presence to its fullness, giving birth to Jesus.

The reign of God is, as noted earlier, the state of affairs wherein God's will is fulfilled. God's reign is contrasted with the reign of human rulers who lord it over others and who let their own petty goals and schemes take control. This is the condition of the world we are in, so full of conflict and warfare and misery. This world of ours is governed not by God's will but by the will of self-centered human beings, with their little egos clashing against one another and thereby hurting and harming one another. We dwell in a wounded world, in a vale of tears, caused by our own human pettiness and self-centeredness. It is in this wounded world, this vale of tears, that Jesus has come, proclaiming that the reign of God is near.

This is the Good News: the reign of God is in your midst, so just open your heart to it, and you will see. Be still, and know.

What happens when that reign of God does come? We pray the prayer that Jesus taught us: *Our Father, who art in heaven, hallowed be thy name. Thy kingdom come; thy will be done on earth as it is in heaven.* Those two items are really referring to the same reality. *Thy kingdom come. Thy will be done on earth as it is in heaven.* When God's will is accomplished both on earth as it is always so in heaven, then that is when the reign of God becomes fully present.

To what does this term the "kingdom of heaven" point? The term "heaven" refers to many things, but it could mean the firmament up there, but we take the term as indicating where God is fully present. That place where God is fully present, which is in contrast with the earth, where there is still an "up there" as opposed to a "down here." In the latter sense, there is a wall of separation between "heaven" (up there) and "earth" (down here), as reflected in the biblical worldview we can glean from this passage. From another angle, "heaven" points to that which is beyond this world, the transcendent realm, that which is on the other side. And yet let us note: Jesus proclaimed that that which is "on the other side" has now come and is in our midst. Luke 17:21 is very significant. "Do not look hither or thither," because that reign that you are seeking is truly in your midst, so just open your eyes and welcome it. It is already right there, closer than you think. Just like *mu.* Those of you who may be working with that koan, this is your hint: it is closer to you than you think. As Augustine exclaimed, when he discovered the presence of God in his own life, *You are more intimate to me than I am to myself.*[3] Just open your eyes and see it, everywhere. But our minds are full of expectations, desires, and ideals of something "out there"

---

[3] Augustine, *Confessions* III, 6:11.

that we think we haven't quite attained yet. We look in a certain direction, expecting whatever it is, and fail to see that it is right here in front of us. This way of sitting in stillness, paying attention at each moment, brings us back to the place where it will appear before us.

I noted previously that I prefer to use the term "kin-dom" rather than "kingdom." The English word "kingdom" is used in a context where there are rulers called kings or absolute monarchs who impose their wills on other people. And other people had to obey, or else off with their heads. That was the image attached to the term "kingdom." Feminist theologians have noted that this image can alienate some because the image of king is one that is far away and male-centered, or patriarchal. Incidentally, for those of us who play chess, however, it is the Queen that is the dominating figure. The Queen is a powerful player that accomplishes the moves that enable the player to win. The King can only move one space at a time, but when the King is in checkmate, the game is over. So the Queen must defend the King. In any case, we now see that the dichotomy between male and female, whereby roles are assigned based on sociological expectations, needs to be overcome. Both the male and female, both the masculine and feminine dimensions are to be seen as aspects of our being human.

In my own usage, I refer to "the reign of God," following Ada María Isasi-Díaz's proposal, using *kin-dom*, as it highlights two important aspects. One is that "the reign of God" is in our midst; it is "akin" to us, intimately tied up with our very being. Another is that as we allow God to reign in our lives, we are able to realize that we all kin to one another, that all beings are bonded together by an intimate kinship, *kin-dom*. We are all kin to one another. When we open our eyes to who we are and hear that acknowledgment, *You are blessed*, we are there in the midst of the kin-dom of God. Looking around, we see that those around us are also blessed in their own unique ways. We are able to celebrate that blessedness with one another in an eternal feast. That image of a feast, a meal, is a prominent one associated with the kin-dom: we are all sharing a meal together, all the members of God's family, gratefully and gloriously basking in God's and in one another's presence, in unending celebration.

This reminds me of a story that I would like to relate again, one that mirrors for us what this "kin-dom" is all about. A certain person dies, and this person's soul is now on the way to the Judgment Place. The question is whether the final destination will be heaven or hell, based on the way this person behaved and lived life on earth. There is a long line of those waiting their turn at judgment, so while waiting in line, this soul notices one of the guardian angels who happens to be loitering around near the waiting line, and asks, "What's it like in hell?" The angel, who had a bit of time to spare and was getting bored with playing the harp anyway, made an offer. "Hey, let me take you to a tour of the place, so you'll see for yourself." The soul agrees, so the angel takes the soul out of the line (asking the others in line to mark that place for the return) through a dark tunnel, and they enter through a portal that has a sign, "The Gate of Hell." They go through the portal, and the soul is ushered in to a big banquet hall where there were many other souls who were consigned to this place. They are all standing around a large table filled with many delicious kinds of food, making everyone's mouth water. They are waiting for the signal when they may start eating. When the signal is finally given, they all come closer to the table to take the food. But what they can use for taking the food are chopsticks placed at the side of the table, measuring about a yard long. (This is an Asian story, hence, chopsticks. If told in a Western culture, perhaps they would have had forks and knives, but also a yard long.) So the hungry souls rush to get their hands on a pair of chopsticks each, grasp the food on the table with these, and try to put the food in their own mouths. But since the chopsticks are too long, the food does not reach their mouths, and just falls to the floor every time they try to take a bite. The souls around the table keep grabbing at more and more food with their chopsticks, and keep trying to put food into their own mouths, but get frustrated each time, just fanning their hunger all the more, and becoming angry and pushing one another aside as they keep trying to feed themselves.

Our visitor soul looks at this scene, and realizes what hell is like. It is a state of unending frustration and dissatisfaction, fanning anger at everyone around, and the irony is that what they are so longing for, which can satisfy their hunger and end their frustration, is right there before them. It is right there before them, but they are not able to access it and get it to where they want it, into their mouths, no matter how much they keep trying, given the yard-long chopsticks they must use.

Our visitor soul is filled with sadness at the sight and asks the angel to be taken back to the place in line, hoping not to be consigned to "that" place when judgment time comes. "In heaven, the chopsticks must be short ones, then," the soul asks the angel as they make their way back. "No, they are just as long. Let me show you." So this time they make their way up through bright clouds, and they hear harp music playing along the way and are allowed entrance to a place with a sign that says "The Pearly Gates." Ushered in to the banquet room, the scene looks somewhat similar to the one just seen below: hungry souls around a large table filled with delicious food, and, surprisingly, similar yard-long chopsticks at the side of the table for use in eating. When the signal to start is given, though, these souls, instead of rushing to grab a pair of chopsticks to get their own food for themselves, seem to be telling one another, "Oh, please go ahead; let me go right after you." They give way to one another, and as one picks up a pair of yard-long chopsticks and takes some food with it, that soul offers it to a neighbor, putting the food into the hungry neighbor's mouth. The neighbor, grateful, takes a pair of chopsticks, picks up some food, and likewise offers it to the other. They continue in this way, using the long chopsticks to offer the food at the table to one another, and to other neighbors, who receive each mouthful with gratitude, and offer some in return to the giver.

In this place called heaven, the soul realizes, everyone is able to partake of the good things given right in front of them, and are satisfied, precisely because they think of one another and give way to each other in fulfilling their need. Their hearts are open to one another, and they see to it that their neighbor is taken care of, and in the process, each one is also taken care of by neighbors. Everyone feasts together, and they all celebrate their being with one another, grateful for the good things they are given all together.

The point of the story speaks for itself in the narrative. The difference between hell and heaven, between eternal doom and participation in the kin-dom, lies in the difference between an ego-centered and self-preoccupied mode of being, and a heart of one that is able to receive and care for one's neighbor. The difference between heaven and hell lies not so much in the external circumstances that befall us in life, but how we comport ourselves through the circumstances that are part of our lot in life. Our entry into the kin-dom of God is marked by the transformation in our own inner attitude and mode of being, overcoming the self-seeking, ego-centered tendencies we find in ourselves, and arriving at a heart open to others in compassion.

We are invited to start from where we are, and from there, enable that kin-dom to be manifest in our own lives, here and now. And in a most natural way, the ripple effect will take place, in a way that will eventually transform this entire world we all live in together, fulfilling the words of Jesus: *the kin-dom of God is in your midst!*

Our sitting practice gives us the inner space to open our eyes and realize and experience that it is truly, really in our midst. A change of heart can happen as we sit in stillness. Or it can happen in some unguarded moment, when we are simply there and present to whatever may be in front of us. And when it does, the whole world now looks entirely different. It is the same old world, with its wounds and with its struggles, and challenges, yet we are now able to see them in an entirely different way. *Blessed are the poor in spirit, for theirs is the kin-dom of heaven.*

This *kin-dom of heaven* can be seen as resonating with the Buddhist notion referred to as the "divine dwelling." This is the place of peace (*santam padam*) that those who tread the path of awakening arrive at. This divine dwelling is described as marked by four characteristics, four "immeasurables," as these are boundless in extent. To recall, they are loving-kindness, compassion, sympathetic joy, and equanimity, described in chapter 1.

Beginning with the last of the four characteristics, the word translated as "equanimity" in English is in Sanskrit *upeksha* (*upekkha* in Pali, the language in which the early Buddhist scriptures were transmitted), which literally means "seeing at close hand," that is, seeing without any obstruction, seeing things "just as they are." It is our capacity, our ability to see things as they are without the obstruction of the subject-object polarity, without the obstruction of our expectations or our images of what we have heard before. It is simply letting each thing be manifest as it is, which thus enables us to take each thing as it is and accept it with peace of mind, realizing that it is just as it is, and not something else. This does not mean, of course, that we are just passive about things, or merely submissive to the status quo, but it means that we are able to discern those things that are beyond our control; we are able to accept them as they are with peace of mind. This state of mind is also conveyed in the well-known Prayer of Serenity. *"Oh God, grant me the serenity to accept what I cannot change, the courage to change the things I can, and the wisdom to know the difference."*

Sympathetic joy (*mudithā* in Pali) refers to the heart that rejoices in the good things that happen to others, the capacity to celebrate with others in their joy, as opposed to the narrow mind that envies others when they find something joyful or wants to have that joy for themselves instead. This attitude is tied up intimately with the other two, loving-kindness, *mettā*, the heart and mind that seeks the well-being of everyone, and compassion (*karunā*), the heart and mind that bears the pain and suffering of others and seeks to alleviate this to the best of one's ability. The word *mettā* comes from a word that means a sense of kinship, friendliness, spiritual bonding. This term is thus readily resonant with the term "kin-dom."

This is where the kin-dom is made manifest: when we acknowledge everyone around us as our own kin, then it is but natural to look at everyone and embrace everyone with the heart of loving-kindness, with that deep aspiration toward the well-being of each and every one, in the best way we can. That is also what assures our well-being, when we seek and do and say and think things toward the well-being of others as the most natural thing to do. It is the heart of a parent who wants only the greatest well-being for his or her own child.

As we realize what it is to dwell in this Divine Dwelling, with the four marks noted above, we realize that there is no longer a barrier between "Self" and "Other"—we are in the realm of kin-dom. An awakened life is all about the embodiment of a life of truly being kin, intimately, with each and every one.

We are able to discern intimations of the *kin-dom of heaven* that is in our midst. These are accessible to us as we simply open our eyes and ears, to see and listen. "To contemplate," a word we use in our Christian tradition, comes from the Greek word *theorein*, which means "to see." To see things in this way, in the Gospel of John, is resonant with *pisteuein*, "to believe." We are given this invitation to live the contemplative life, to live life with our eyes wide open in a way that what is, is acknowledged and welcomed for what it is, "the way things are." In seeing that, we are able to discern our interconnected-ness with all, which grounds that sense of kinship with every-one, which in turn gushes forth with loving-kindness toward each and every one. It is this contemplative heart, the capacity to see things as they are, which enables us to also share in the woundedness of all our fellow beings and enables us also to share in the joys that others are experiencing, as an aspect of our being kin to them.

The kin-dom of God and the kin-dom of heaven are syn-onymous terms. If there is any meaning to this term "God" that we use in our human language, there must be some con-nection with these intimations that we experience as we sit and listen in silence. Let us then continue to sit and listen and let that kin-dom of God be fully manifest and move us so that our life is now acknowledged as a gift meant to realize the kin-dom of heaven on this earth.

Blessed Are the Pure of Heart

Let us take another Beatitude as a pointer to direct us to our true home.

Blessed are the pure of heart, for they shall see God.

A Zen talk is not a "lecture" or discourse that deals with concepts, nor is it meant to give listeners new ideas or information about things. It is offered rather as a set of pointers to something important in Zen, especially the core of each listener's being, the "heart" or "mind." These are two alternative English words used to render the Chinese character *hsin*, or the Japanese *kokoro*. The one who gives a talk in Zen is always pointing to each of you as you sit there with openness to listen in the silence, breathing in and breathing out, telling each and every one, "This is about you. Listen as if you were alone in the universe hearing this." So you are invited to listen wholeheartedly, not getting lost in the words or concepts that happen to be used in the discourse, but letting those words and concepts point you back to that place that you yourself are seeking so earnestly to arrive at, or better, to return to, and find your peace of mind, find your own true home.

Let that be the attitude with which you read these words in this book also: "It's all about you." But not just the little "you" that you imagine as your individual identity, as distinguished from everyone else, but that You that is intimately connected to everyone and everything, and is also called to embrace everyone and everything as yourself: the big You, the True Self that you are, "the Big Mind," as one Zen master called it.

The first word we have looked at as our pointer is "blessed." Let us keep returning to what we may have glimpsed in taking that pointer as a guide. *You are blessed.*

And that's you. Blessed are you, indeed. So if you can spend your entire day just basking in that word, set this book aside, and just do that. And not just even this day, the next three or four days, and as long as you live: just taste that, and just immerse yourself in it, and you have what you need for a life-time. *You are blessed.* You are blessed, and that is so for all time. Truly that is our eternal destiny—to live that original blessing that we were given as we were called out of nothingness into being and to live that to the fullest extent, namely, without limits, in infinity. So we can spend our whole lives tasting the blessedness that we are. Breathing in—how blessed it is that we can live and receive this breath; breathing out—how blessed it is that our whole being can receive the blessing and then respond in giving back our whole being, blessing everything around us in return.

> *Blessed are the pure of heart, for they shall see God.*

Every time I hear this passage, what comes to me is another passage that for me summarizes the entire biblical message. It is from the opening lines of the Letter to the Ephesians, right after the author's salutation.

> *Blessed be the God and father of our lord Jesus Christ, who has blessed us in Christ with every spiritual blessing in the heavens. God chose us before the world began to be holy and blameless in God's sight, full of love. (Eph. 1:3–4)*

Again the opening is *Blessed.* The author (traditionally thought to be Paul the Apostle, but, from other indications noted by scholars, may have been someone else), having experienced that blessedness and having encountered Christ the Risen One, is bubbling with joy at that experience and real-ization. And his exclamation out of that bubbling joy, para-phrased, is "Blessed be the One who created us all as blessed! Blessed be the One whom we can address as Father, Mother, who is the source of this life of us all, the source of who *I am* and the source of everything that is intimately connected with all that *I am*." This is his way of responding to that blessing that he himself has deeply experienced, which he realizes as having been bestowed on us all since even before creation, before the beginning of time. This is an exuberant exclamation of *blessing upon blessing*. The original blessing was bestowed on us, calling us out of nothingness into being, and then we realized, "How blessed it is, just *to be*, and *to be just as we are!*"

And so we are called to live our life fully, just going on living and experiencing that blessing in all that happens to us, and giving that blessing back to all that we encounter from day to day. "Blessed are You, O Source of all that there is! Blessed is all that there is! Blessed are the trees, the birds, the sun, the moon, every blade of grass, every little particle in this universe!" And it is so, because everything, just as it is, is simply a manifestation and reflection of that original blessing with which we have been blessed with from all eternity.

Recall that many Jewish prayers begin with this exultation in blessing. *Baruch Atah Adonai Eloheinu Melech Ha'Olam*— Blessed are You, Holy One, who reigns all over the earth!

Our human life is one of continually receiving blessings from all and giving back blessings to all in return for the blessings that we have received. So we can just let this sink in and realize that for all eternity there is nothing else we need; everything we could ever need or want is already given to us. With every breath, breathing in and out, with every step, one foot forward, the next foot forward, with every turn, with every sensation, with every sight, sound, smell, taste, touch, all blessing upon blessing.

> . . . *who has blessed us in Christ with every spiritual blessing in heavens.*

We are blessed "in Christ," which means that we have been brought into the intimate family that shares the very life of God, in Christ, God's own Beloved. It is God's own goodness, the infinite goodness that God is, that we are now called to be a part of. Our lives are rooted in that very blessedness that is the origin of the universe. That is beyond anything that we ever imagine or think of or grasp as a concept. So let us sit still and dwell on this mystery.

Who is this source of all? And what is this origin that we are talking about? We don't know; nobody knows. Or you might want to say, "Only God knows." And yet we are right there in the midst of it. We are immersed in that infinite bounty, basking in it for all eternity. In sitting still, we are invited to just taste that and see for ourselves, with every breath. "Taste and see the goodness of the Lord," the psalm invites us. And not just with every breath; but when the bell rings, blessed is that sound, blessed is that bell. As I stand up again and begin to walk, blessed it is, and now with every step, how blessed is that step, and how blessed it is that I am able to walk, one blessed step after blessed step. Some of us who may have had some physical difficulties in walking may be able to appreciate this more than others, namely, the fact that we can walk, taking this step, and that step, and so on.

A few years ago, I was on a retreat in Germany with some of our Zen brothers and sisters, and while going up some stairs in the monastery where we were having the retreat, I slipped, twisted my ankle, and fell down, rolling down the stairs. I was in severe pain and was brought immediately to a clinic in town. After examining my leg, the doctor told me I had broken the fibula. Since I was due to fly back to the United States a few days after that, they decided not to do anything but just put a cast around the leg with the broken bone. I was given a plane seat where I could lift up the leg that was in a cast all throughout the flight.

And so when I came back to Dallas and went to a hospital here, the doctor looked at it, and said, "No, you don't need surgery. It's broken, but if we just keep it together so that it doesn't get further agitated and dislocated, then it will heal on its own." So for three or four months, one leg was in a cast. Since my other leg was functioning, I could still go about, be driven back and forth from school, but I needed crutches to help me walk.

With one leg in a cast, even one step was already a big effort. And so I went through that period, going about my daily life and work. To make a long story short, it was for me a marvelous experience of experiencing my body in the process of healing, moment after moment, day after day. It was an awesome experience, as I imagined those broken bones and how they were gradually being brought back together through some mysterious force that enveloped them, enveloped my whole body, enveloped the whole universe, toward healing and wholeness. I was just taking every day as it came, in my life at home with family, taking my meals, and also preparing my classes, giving lectures, reading and grading papers, and so on, going about life as usual. This went on for about three or four months, and when I went to the doctor at the appointed time after that, I was told that the leg was now healed, so the cast was taken off, and lo and behold, it was back to where it was before. I could now walk again without any crutch, without any pain. That three- or four-month period brought home to me in a most immediate and intimate way that things happen in our own body, and all around us, without our fully realizing them, that there is a mysterious power that brings us toward wholeness, bringing us to healing, as it did to my left leg over that period.

The fact that we can take a step without feeling pain or without having to go through the effort of using crutches—we take this for granted as "the way it's supposed to be." And yes, it's true, that's the way it is "supposed to be," but all in the light of this wondrous mystery that we are what we are, and things are the way they are—*Blessed are we in all this!*

Let us taste and see each moment: how blessed we are, how surrounded we are with so many blessed things, and the only appropriate response is gratitude, and our whole lives will not be enough to be able to respond to that adequately. But we try; that's all we can do really; respond with gratitude to everything that we have been given.

Theologians remind us that if God withdrew the support, even for a moment, that keeps us being as we are, we would all vanish in an instant. So the very fact that we continue here breathing in and out, stepping this step, that step, is a direct indication that we are enveloped in the divine embrace.

> *God chose us before the world began to be holy and blameless in God's sight, full of love.*

God chose us before the world began, to be holy and blameless, beheld in divine light, overflowing in divine love. "Full of love" is the translations for "*in agape*," immersed in that *agape*. And what is that *agape*? From the Greek, it is "outpouring love," that love that seeks no return but simply pours out for its own sake, and it is that love that called us out of nothingness into being; we are receiving that love, and again the natural response is to simply love back.

That makes me recall an important part of the Spiritual Exercises that I was privileged to partake of when I was a Jesuit. In the twenty-five years of my Jesuit life, I had the opportunity to undergo the full thirty-day retreat three times. After having undergone the first full-scale thirty-day Ignatian retreat in the first year of having entered the Jesuits, every year after that, I would undertake an eight-day version. In our day-to-day schedule outside of the retreat, the normal practice was to take one hour of each day in contemplative practice, taking a theme from the Spiritual Exercises.

Contemplative practice was thus part of the life of those called to the Society of Jesus. Of course, in other religious congregations there are other ways of contemplation, but in the Spiritual Exercises that I was privileged to partake of, the key, or the crowning point is at the end, called the "Contemplation on Divine Love." There are several facets of the exercises on God's love, so let me just introduce some of them.

The first facet is that love is not just one-sided, but it presupposes communion. Love is given, and love is then given back in return. We are invited to realize and directly experience that we are already being given that love in full measure, so now an invitation is offered to simply return that love as we continue living our entire life. A prayer of Ignatius called "*Suscipe*" in Latin is introduced here: "Take and receive all that I have, all that I am, all my will, all my memory, all my being, and let it be at the service of your will, according to your Love."

If we are able to embody this prayer in our lives, and let it sink into every pore of our being, our life then becomes no longer one in which we are seeking this and that, wanting this and wanting that, because we know that deep within we've been given so much already, all that we need, and all we could ever want for our entire lifetime. So now we simply direct our life to simply giving back that love we continue to receive in bountiful ways, in whatever way that we are called to do so, to whomever we encounter. That is the mode of life we are called to. That is the first point in this contemplation of God's love. We have been given so much, so we give back, and live the rest of our life in that mode of giving back.

Another facet that I'd like to introduce is Ignatius's invitation to just sit there with open eyes and consider something around us in a concrete and particular manner. For example, take any inanimate object—it could be a pebble, a stump of a tree, or even the floor we are sitting on, anything that is immediately there right in front of us. Now consider how that pebble or tree or the floor in itself is made up of so many intricate elements, atoms, molecules, subatomic particles that are in dynamic motion in minuscule scales that escape our line of sight. Ignatius did not know about atoms or electrons, but now our knowledge of the way the universe works has become intricately complex. Science, especially cutting-edge science, rather than wiping out any trace of mystery and letting everything become clear and self-evident, reveals to us all the more how mystery abounds, how we are surrounded by so many unknowns. We know from scientific discoveries how even one little pebble is a manifestation of so many intricate laws of the universe, and we can also affirm based on these scientific perspectives how one pebble embraces the whole universe.

I recall a book published in 1975 titled *The Tao of Physics* by Fritjof Capra. The message of that book can still be an eye-opener for many of us. Research in the physical sciences has continued to advance since then, and the findings only confirm the general directions that Capra already laid out in that book. The findings of the physical sciences are seen to be congruent with what the ancient sages of the East had already realized, namely how everything is interconnected in the universe and how one little material element, like a pebble, is made up of complicated dynamic movements of electrons and all kinds of subatomic particles that show us a marvelously construed universe where every element is intimately interconnected with everything else. I'm not up to date on the terminology. Although I began college with a declared major in physics, I got deflected into philosophy, which eventually led me to the seminary. But I can nostalgically recall how physics was my first love, which I am drawn to once again in these waning years of my life. Just seeing how every material object, every material thing, every pebble, already manifests the intricate and intimate interconnection of everything in the cosmos, into that web of kinship that bonds us all, boggles the mind, and invites us to just behold in awe.

Ignatius had seen that as he undertook his own spiritual exercises, even though he didn't have the scientific knowledge that could spell out all the theoretical aspects that humans in more recent times would be able to discover and articulate more systematically with mathematical equations and all the technical paraphernalia involved. In the simplicity of his heart, purified through the process he had gone through in his path spelled out in the Spiritual Exercises, he saw the Divine Presence that is contained in each pebble, each grain of sand. This is the mystery of God present in our midst, the mystery of God's love already revealed in the grain of sand or the pebble, and in each and every element of this universe.

And Ignatius guides us to go further and look at other things around us. He had in mind what he learned from the cosmology of his time, which can be described as a "hierarchy of beings," where different things manifest different levels of being within this hierarchy, from inanimate objects to vegetative life to animal life and then to humans and spiritual beings. He invites us thus to contemplate the next level, like a flower or a blade of grass, or a tree, something endowed with a form of life in the plant world. We are now looking at something that manifests the mystery of life, and there is a new set of relations that relate to all life. We are invited to sit and breathe and consider the mystery that manifests itself to us in this tree.

We are invited to allow it to take us to that same realization of being wrapped in immense love, which gives life to this form of life we are contemplating before us.

At the next level, we consider the animal world. It could be your household pet, your cat or dog. Our beloved pet can teach us about the mystery of the universe. Let us sit and listen, and be immersed in the love that exudes from this four-legged friend of ours. There is a pet Yorkie named Pepe, owned by a dear friend and her family, who, as she emphatically affirms, with all of his antics and yelps and funny movements, teaches her the meaning of true unconditional love on a daily basis.

And then Ignatius invites us to consider a particular human being as the subject of our contemplative practice. Consider one of your loved ones. It could be your mother, your father, an uncle or aunt, a grandparent, a sibling. Just recall one human being that you care for or who has cared for you, and let yourself be in that person's presence. Let the entire being of that person "speak" to you in the silence. Bask in the unconditional love that this person has given or continues to give you, wherever he or she may be, still alive or already passed on. Sit with that, for as many periods of contemplative practice as necessary. Just *be* with that person in the midst of that period of silence, and let that person's presence in your life tell you of the many angles of unconditional love that you are immersed in since birth up to this point of your journey, and on through this earthly life and beyond.

Through these various exercises, Ignatius invites us to simply taste and experience that which we are already surrounded with, wrapped in, immersed in, right from the start. So there are these various angles that we could take to be able to really appreciate the fact that we are enveloped in God's love. *You are blessed.*

The contemplative exercises recommended above may thus help us appreciate and experience what this beatitude conveys to us: *Blessed are the pure of heart, for they shall see God.*

For They Shall See God

We are looking at the Beatitudes as our pointer to the source of the living waters, where we may drink and never thirst again, as Jesus offered the Samaritan woman at the well (John 4:13).

Blessed are the pure of heart, for they shall see God.

Let us continue our contemplative practice considering this text. What is it to be "pure of heart"? The centuries-old tradition of Zen practice, centered on sitting still and dwelling attentively in the here and now, gives us a constant reminder that what we are talking about is not something "out there," some object, some ideal, some goal to be accomplished through our efforts, but rather, it is right here before us, in our midst. A Zen talk is offered as a way of pointing to the innermost core of being of each and every one who is there to listen. So we are invited to listen (or to read) with full attentiveness, not letting our mind be swept away by ideas and images, but letting it come back to the here and now. As noted earlier, "It's all about you." *Yes, you!*

"*Pure of heart*"—that's you. "Nah," you may be tempted to say, "how can it be little old me? I am just an ordinary human being, with my own issues to work on, with all my struggles and ups and downs in life, with all the narrowness and selfishness that keep coming up in different ways and messing up my life and that of others. How can that be referring to me?" If you are able to identify with that "objection," please listen again.

Christian theologians since the Middle Ages sought to articulate this immense and awesome mystery referred to as "God," using different words and concepts that they knew could never be up to the task. One widely accepted formulation affirms that "God is that than which nothing greater can be conceived."

This is meant to remind us that if our mind comes up with an idea or concept and identifies it with "God," then it is no longer God, since that idea or concept would have "pegged" God into something definable. In short, the very term is meant to point us to something beyond what our minds can grasp.

Another expression relevant for us here is the reference to God as "pure be-ing." I use a hyphen to indicate that the word "be-ing" is to be distinguished from "being" as used in ordinary language, a word which refers to things that exist, those objects we can point to all around us accessible to our sense perception. A grammatically awkward way of putting it is that God is "pure *to be*." We can agree that what is referred to as "God" is not, and cannot be a "being" in that sense, even if we say "the highest being" or even "Supreme Being," because that would reduce God to a being among other beings, albeit thought of as the "highest" one or the "supreme" one.

So we are dealing with something elusive here, which can easily lead us to fall into a conceptual trap. Note how Paul Tillich used the term "Ground of Being" in referring to God, with an acknowledgment that God is on a totally different plane from the beings that we are familiar with in our experience. There is much more that we can say in this regard, but I will cut it short for now, and get to the point I would like to convey for this particular theme of our contemplative practice. *Blessed are the pure of heart, for they shall see God.*

What is to be seen by the pure of heart? That pure "to be" is something that we can never grasp with our mind. And yet, lo and behold, the very fact that you, I, this pebble, that mountain, the clouds, the sky, we all "be," in the distinctive and unique way that each of us "be's" (I am deliberately going beyond grammatical rules here) is grounded in our participation in that pure "*to be*."

Taking another angle, I, as a subjective conscious being, can acknowledge and say, "I am," in the unique and particular way that "I am." The fact that each of us, you (the reader), me (the one writing this), and everyone else can say "I am" each in one's own individual and unique way. This is the very manifestation of our participation as we each are, *"just as I am,"* in that infinite "to be." Let us taste that as we sit in stillness, in the depths of the silence.

If you would like to dwell on that point throughout the day, throughout your life as a matter of fact, then you may realize that *that itself* is enough to nourish us for whatever we may need for the rest of our lives. Just bask in the fact of *I am*, letting yourself be launched into the depth and breadth and height of all that this entails, before it turns into "I am a man" or "I am seventy years old," or "I am this" or "I am that," that is, before the boundless, limitless, and timeless *I am* is solidified into something objectifiable and identifiable as a particular thing or person.

To listen in the stillness for the reverberations of *I am* and all that this entails is a direct way of experiencing our participation, our immersion, in that pure "to be," that infinite and boundless horizon that we call God in the Christian tradition, yet Whom we also address as You, Holy One, Father, Mother, Lover, that One Who embraces us in love that we may experience in the midst of that silence, and the One Whom we embrace in our heart as we respond to love in embracing back the world to offer ourselves in its service. The pure "*to be*"—that is what we are all immersed in, that is what we all share in, and that is what we all are in our fullness. To be "pure of heart" is to realize our participation in this pure "to be." So let us come back to that pure "to be" that we are, and we will realize that all we can "do" is to simply continue basking in this "to be" our entire lives, letting all our thoughts, words, and actions, all that we "do," simply flow from the abundance of this "to be."

We recall that when Moses was on Mount Sinai and encountered the burning bush and received a message that he was to lead his people to freedom, he asked, "Who is it who is commanding me to do all of these things for my people?" The answer he received, in Hebrew, is *ehyeh asher ehyeh*, which biblical translators have rendered as "I am who am," or "I will be as I will be." Or more simply, "*I am*." This encounter was a very powerful experience that defined Moses' entire life from that point on, as he realized that he was no longer just this given individual human being with his own little ambitions and purposes in life, with his particular background and upbringing, with all the particular memories he carried up to that point, including the guilt that he may have felt for having killed an Egyptian, and of all the things that he was carrying with him as part of the bundle of his historical existence. All of that just melted away in the face of this pure *I am*. And from that point on, he was simply a vessel, an instrument that conveyed the message of this *I am* to whomever he met, and all his actions were simply particular ways of allowing this *I am* to unfold in the various events and encounters of his life.

That is the same calling each person is called to undertake in his or her personal life, including all the particulars, the given qualities and gifts, as well as the limitations. As we allow this *I am* to become the pervading power that undergirds our entire life and our entire being, we understand ourselves, in all the particularities of our lives, as gifts of that pure "to be." Then the concrete mode of being from here on becomes the particularization of that "to be" in our day-to-day life.

We are invited to sit in silence, and to immerse ourselves in the vast and boundless ocean of "to be," and to know that with this, there is nothing else we could ever want, there is nothing else we could ever need in life. We can just continue our lives keeping ourselves dipped in that ocean, and immersed in the living waters that flow from there. Whatever we would need in life would come from that abundant source, in whatever situation we may encounter from here on.

We are invited first to accept that concrete reality that we are as we find ourselves. Accept your concrete individuality, and having done that, then you may also realize, *you are blessed just as you are.*

We human beings are given the capacity to reflect on this "to be" in a way that, for example, the trees and the flowers or cats and dogs or even this wood, are not. There's this so-called self-reflexiveness that our human mode of being is given as a gift. Now that is precisely what enables us to acknowledge that fact of "to be," that "I am," but it is also that which puts it under a cloud of darkness, a cloud that comes with the discriminating thoughts of our discursive intellect. When we just say "I am" and open our eyes around us, we intuitively see that those others are also included in "I am." I look around and see the lilies of the fields, the trees, the flowers, the pebbles. They just are. They are also embraced in that "I am." And in being what they are, as they are, they already reflect the glory of that pure "to be," that pure *I am* that we call God, just as they are. We too are able to reflect the glory of God, just as we are.

But the discriminating mind tells us, "But these other things different from me; they are not me; they are other to me." So this human mode of reflexive self-awareness leads to this possibility of dividing or shutting off our little "I am" from the "I am" of others. But if in that capacity we are given we just focus that "I am" in our little "I," then the glory of God gets covered up with that little "I" that focuses on itself and shuts out the vast horizon of the boundless "to be." This is what happened to Adam and Eve, when they gave more importance to their individual "I" as they desired "the fruit of the tree of the knowledge of good and evil." In other words, the discriminating mind prods us, "I want to know this"; "I want to be able to decide what I want for myself and what I don't"; "I want the power that this kind of knowledge of discriminating things can bring," that is, the power that the knowledge of good and evil brings. In so doing, I block the opening that enables me to stay in communion with the pure "I AM" that underlies all things that exist in this universe, and shut off my narrow little "I am" from everything else.

Insofar as this little "I" secluded from the boundless "I AM" reigns in our lives, we are blocking the infinite capacity that is the totality of ourselves as enveloped by the boundless "I am." We have fallen from grace.

When we recognize this, what then is our task as human beings? One way to put this is that we are now called to let that little "I am" open up again to the big "I AM." My late teacher, the Jesuit spiritual director Father Thomas Hand, SJ, had an expression that he repeated time and again about what Zen practice was about. "It is about moving from the ego to the *we-go*." In other words, in our practice of sitting in still- ness and allowing ourselves to go deep into the silence, we are enabled to see through this little "I am," and in doing so, we open our hearts and realize that we are all embraced by that vast and boundless "I AM." That is what we are called to really embody in this life: this is our "role," our particular and unique place within the big scheme of things. It is to let the big Self, the *we-go* that Father Hand spoke about, become the ground and basis of everything that I think, say, and do as an individual human being. So as we put that little "I am" in its place, that is, in the light of the big "I AM," we are able to acknowledge our individual gifts as well as our limitations and realize that each of us has his or her own unique gifts and limitations. So we find ourselves in good company with everyone, and we are thus enabled and empowered to accept everyone around us *just as they are*, as we now are able to see them in the light of the big "I AM" that also embraces my own individual existence. Everyone is simply a reflection of that same "I AM" just as they are.

The message here is this: accept yourself just as you are, with all of your struggles and issues and weaknesses. And in accepting yourself, you're simply agreeing to the fact that *you are already accepted* by the entire universe, just as you are. So don't block that movement of the universe accepting you as you are, thinking, "But I am an imperfect, troubled, vulnerable human being full of faults." Yes, you may be, but you are accepted just as you are, no ifs, no buts. So just allow that to sink in as you sit there in the silence, and you will experience the great freedom of just being yourself. And with that, even those aspects we think are our gaps or limitations can be gifts. So let us then bask in that acceptance.

Jesus invited the disciples: "Behold the lilies of the field, see how they bloom." They never worry about whether they have little stains of dust, because these would just blow away anyway. Just let us learn from each and every thing that simply is there, just as they are, reflecting the glory of that infinite source of our being, that boundless, timeless, infinite "I am." And as we do so, we also acknowledge that even in my own little way, I can reflect that also. I am a reflection of *that* also. So let us accept that we are accepted, and that will open the floodgates of the Infinite to enter into our lives. The rest of our life can then be an unfolding of that infinite horizon, allowing it to be embodied and made fully manifest in every event and every encounter in this earthly life of ours.

My teacher Yamada Kōun gives an account of his own experience of opening to this infinite and boundless "I am."

He wrote of how he was riding a train and reading a passage by Dōgen that said, *"The mind is no other than mountains and rivers, the great wide earth, the sun, the moon, the stars."* And that passage just jumped out at him and he realized, "That's it!" What is referred to as "mind" here, *hsin* in Chinese, or *kokoro* in Japanese, is the True Self, our Original Face, the "true nature" that we are, as understood in the Zen tradition. To see this "true nature" is to come to true awakening. The question, "What is the mind?" is the same as the question, "What or who am I?" Yamada Kōun Rōshi experienced the *fact* that was behind the expression from Dōgen and was awakened.

He came to the realization that this "mind," this "self," this "I" that we refer to in our discursive language, is truly, truly, *nothing but* the mountains, rivers, the great wide earth, the sun, the moon, the stars, in short, each and every thing that exists in the whole universe. To put it in terms of what we were looking at earlier, our "True Self" is everything that is a partaker of this "to be," and there is no single thing that exists in this universe that is separate from this "to be" that has now come to be manifest in me.

I may be saying too much here already that may block your own path to opening your eyes, but all of this is offered as a pointer to that source of living water.

"Blessed are the pure of heart, for they shall see God." Again, what is there to "see"? If we think that God is some magnificent thing that we can see out there, some magnificent being or Being that we can now recognize and bow down to in adoration, then there is a conceptual disjoint here. Whatever we can objectify is no longer the living God, but an idol that we have constructed in our own little mind. As long as we think that we have it, then we already miss it. God is beyond anything that we can ever imagine. Again, our medieval theologians are united in that, that God is that beyond which we can

ever conceive, greater than that which can ever be conceived. So you think, "Ah, that's it!"—and we need to be reminded, no, it is beyond that.

But in all of these efforts and endeavors, we are invited to just come back to that purity of heart that we originally have been, this original blessing we are endowed with right from the start. You are good. You are beloved. You are, just as you are. And you partake in this boundless "*I am,*" as you are. So as we really hear that in the depths of our hearts and melt into it, and therein find the "ground of our be-ing," to borrow from Paul Tillich, then what emerges is a view, no longer from the small "I am," but from that infinite ground of all that proclaims *I am.* We see our little "I am" in its place in the light of this big picture, and we are able to accept that little "I am" as the gift that we have received from the universe, that we can now also give back to the rest of the universe, in loving service to all.

Finally, what is there "to see" when it is said, "Blessed are the pure of heart, for they shall see God"? Frankly, there is nothing that we can adequately say, or ever think of or imagine, by way of answering this directly. But yet the gospel passage says, "*for they shall see God.*" How can we understand this? Let us take some hints from Zen tradition. In Zen, the experience of awakening is expressed as "seeing one's true nature," "seeing one's True Self." Awakening is seeing what or who you truly are. Not just as an aspect or part of it, but *just as you are.* Now in the Japanese language, when someone explains something to you and you "see" what the person is conveying, you say, "*naru hodo,*" translated in English as "Oh, I see." "*Naru hodo*" literally means "It becomes exactly." What was not seen before is now seen clearly for what it is, and so "it becomes exactly" just as it is. This is a daily expression, *naru hodo,* that people use lightly in casual conversations. "That's it, exactly." So that's what we are invited to experience, that moment of "that's it, exactly."

The Orthodox tradition has upheld and preserved an important aspect of the Christian message, which somehow got lost in a lot of the theological tradition of Western Christianity. This is the theme of "*theosis*," translated as "deification," or "divinization," as the ultimate destiny of the human being. God became human so that humans may become God. That infinite, boundless mystery that we refer to as God, which is beyond everything in this created universe yet is also that which is the ground of this created universe, has now willingly assumed this bodily being of ours, this flesh, this earth. And in doing so, through this event that is called the Incarnation, literally, "becoming flesh," we are able to open our eyes to our true and ultimate destiny, that is, to come back to our home at the heart of that Infinite Mystery, in that boundless and infinite and pure "*to be*."

Let us take this message in all simplicity and allow it to sink in as we sit in stillness. Western Christianity has become preoccupied with human fallenness, on the doctrine of "original sin," and that has served to sidetrack this important message of our ultimate destiny as emphasized in the Eastern Orthodox tradition. Let us just take this invitation to come back and hear the words again. *Be still, and know . . . I AM.*

And in the very resonance of that, through each and every participant of that "I AM" in the universe, we see how our ultimate destiny is to sing the glories of that *I AM,* vast and boundless, and never-ending. Indeed, *Blessed are the pure of heart, for they shall see God.*

Conclusion

Zen and the Bible:
Experiencing a Loving Presence

When our sons, Florian and Benjamin, were about three and two years old, Maria and I would read stories to them before bedtime and then pray with them and then tuck them in. Such are indeed precious moments that remain in a parent's heart even as their children grow into adulthood. On a good number of those occasions I recall when we chose a Bible story to read to them, and toward the conclusion of the story, one of them would blurt out spontaneously in a cute childlike voice, "And God gave them all a BIG hug. The end!" And the four of us would then all burst into laughter, give one another a hug and a kiss, and the boys would then be tucked into bed for the night.

I recall this treasure from our family memory in concluding this volume taking Zen practice, the practice of simply being still and opening one's heart in that stillness, as a way to "taste and see" the core message of the Bible. One of my New Testament professors in the seminary during the early years of my Jesuit formation likened the Bible to a "love letter from God, addressed to all of us human beings." Indeed, for Christians, the Bible is the Word of God that reveals to us the divine plan of salvation, the grand design God has in store for all. The short form of this core message can be summed up in the words found in Mark 1:11: "*You are my Beloved, in whom I am well pleased.*"

My Zen teacher, Master Yamada Koun, on several occasions during his Zen talks at the small Zendo where he taught in Kamakura, Japan, repeatedly emphasized that words and concepts are never able to capture what Zen is all about. Zen is about a transformative experience that sheds light on one's entire being and on the entire universe, a never-ending path that continues through a journey of a lifetime and beyond. As a Buddhist, he acknowledged that the words and concepts he used in leading and teaching those who came to him for guidance derived from the Buddhist tradition. He urged his Zen students first and foremost to immerse themselves in Zen practice in a way that they could truly experience that realm that goes beyond words and concepts, and learn to embody it in their lives in the world. There were also a good number of those who had come for his guidance from other countries, including countries in Europe, North America, and Asia. There were those who came from non-Buddhist backgrounds, including Jewish, and Christian (Roman Catholic and Protestant) who sat in many Zen retreats with him over the years. He especially encouraged persons who came from non-Buddhist backgrounds, who had delved deeply into Zen and come to a point of being truly transformed by it and able to embody the Zen way in their own lives, to explore ways of articulating their Zen life and experience to those within their own religious traditions. He thus encouraged those from the Jewish tradition to mine their own Jewish scriptures to find language that could point to those realms that Zen practice opens up, and those from Christian traditions to do the same with their own Bible.

This volume, derived from talks offered at Zen retreats wherein many participants were familiar with or at home in Christian scriptures, is one small way of taking up Master Yamada Koun's invitation, to explore the Bible for ways that can point us toward paths that merge with the Zen path.

We began with the invitation from Psalm 46:10, which is the same invitation Zen practice offers to all: Be still. The threefold structure of Zen practice, that is, taking a posture conducive to stillness, paying attention to one's breath, and allowing the mind to be calm and present in the here and now, is the concrete way Zen unpacks and unfolds this way of being still. The ensuing chapters offered passages and phrases from the Bible that seek to articulate what wells up out of the depths of the stillness.

This book is offered to all spiritual seekers but especially keeps in mind those who regard and accept the Bible as the Word of God (in the different modes in which this may be understood). It highlights key passages that may serve as pointers toward a living encounter with the Holy One, an experience of a Loving Presence in our midst. To one who reads it with the eyes of the heart, the Bible can open a horizon that may transform one's entire life. The invitation is given: Take and read!

Appendix:
*Other Fingers Pointing to the Moon**

⟫—⊶—◯—⊷—⟪

An Interview with
Zen Master Ruben L. F. Habito

Ruben L. F. Habito is a master in the Sanbo Zen lineage, the founding teacher of Maria Kannon Zen Center in Dallas, Texas, and a professor of world religions at Southern Methodist University's Perkins School of Theology. He is also a former Jesuit priest, and as a young ecclesiastic he was sent from his native Philippines to Japan, where he encountered Zen and entered formal training under Yamada Kōun Rōshi, with whom he studied for eighteen years. Discovering Zen was epiphanic for Habito ("it pointed to a realm beyond language"), and koan study became for him a profound foil to the Spiritual Exercises of Saint Ignatius, a set of meditations and devotional practices for Jesuits that Habito had been practicing since entering the order. During his time in Kamakura, the seat of Sanbo Zen, a fusion of Rinzai and Soto traditions formerly called Sanbo Kyodan, Habito met Maria Reis, who became his wife and the mother of their two sons. (Habito left the Jesuits but continues a deep engagement with the religion.)

---

* Reprinted from *Tricycle: The Buddhist Review* (Summer 2014).

In 1989 Habito and Reis moved to Dallas, where Habito founded Maria Kannon, named for the Virgin Mary and Kwan Yin (Guanyin), the bodhisattva of compassion (Kannon in Japanese), two figures who became inexorably linked in seventeenth- and eighteenth-century Japan, when Christianity was banned; Christian practitioners found a worthy manifestation of Mary in the veneration of the bodhisattva, who became known as Maria Kannon. Habito is the author of several books on the relationship between Christianity and Zen practice, among them *Healing Breath: Zen for Christians and Buddhists in a Wounded World* and *Living Zen, Loving God*, both from Wisdom Books.

I first met Ruben in 1990, just one year after he arrived in Dallas from Japan. I was a student at Perkins School of Theology and in the discernment process for the priesthood in the Episcopal Church in the Diocese of West Texas. Ruben had me from the moment he began his required class, "Religion in Global Perspective," with a few minutes of silence. For the duration of the semester, I was part of a small group that met in Ruben's office and breathed, and we visited the place he and his students were using as a zendo and breathed some more.

It was nearly a decade later that my own practice began shifting from a focus on passage meditation to attention to the breath and pure silence. But I was floating around without any guidance. So I made an appointment to see Ruben, and when we met, in the middle of the public gathering area of the Annual Meeting of the American Academy of Religion, he gave me the koan "Mu" while we sat at a plastic table, surrounded by academics and religious scholars of all stripes. Over time, working with Ruben has radically altered how I imagine Jesus guiding his disciples. I hear the parables as koans now, solved not by reason but by action. A Samaritan cares for an injured man: "Show me that!" The first will be last, and the last will be first: "Show me that!"

True to form, Ruben took the lead in commencing our interview, first by asking that "we take a few minutes of silence together," and then by saying, "So we can begin. Ask me questions that will open our conversation."

—*Jane Lancaster Patterson*

How did it all start? What led you to Zen when you were living in Japan as a young seminarian?

My Jesuit spiritual director then, Father Thomas Hand, was studying Zen with a master in Kamakura, and he encouraged me to check it out. I just plunged right in and found it very nourishing and very resonant with what I had learned from my Jesuit spiritual formation. It emphasized the more contemplative aspects rather than the discursive and meditative kinds of things that the Ignatian Exercises, which I had been practicing for six or seven years, are known for. Zen became a way for me to come back to that place of silence, no words, and just find a sense of belonging to the universe.

What kind of training did you receive from your teacher, Yamada Rōshi?

Yamada gave me the basic guideline on just sitting in a very simple way, but it didn't stop at that. There is a whole program of koan training in our Sanbo Zen tradition that guides a person deeper and deeper into the intricacies of the spiritual path. Yamada Rōshi gave me the confidence that I could remain within my Christian context and practice and at the same time really enter into Zen with full commitment.

So he was open to students from other religious traditions?

Yes. His teacher, Yasutani Hakuun Rōshi, had a different view of Christians coming to Zen. He said you have to check your religion at the door and really come with an open and empty mind to be able to receive the benefits of Zen.

My teacher, Yamada Koun, instead of telling Christians to "check your religion at the door," said, "Just come and sit and be still and follow the guidelines of Zen." He realized that it was not so much the religious tradition that needed to be put aside but the concepts that people with a religious background are attached to. He felt there were certain terms in the Christian tradition like *God, Holy Spirit,* and so on that had enough power in them to point to an experience that is beyond concepts.

Was there any conflict for you in bringing the two practices together in your own life?

I needed to go through a struggle for about ten or twelve years to sort out theological concepts—to weed out the conceptual accretions—and see what in the Christian tradition really leads to a genuine experience but is caged in Christian vocabulary or doctrinal terms. I experienced a very liberating affirmation that what unites us *is* the experience.

Some Christians may claim that you jumped ship when you started Zen practice in earnest, and on the other hand, some Buddhists may say you are only dabbling in Zen so long as you remain a Christian So let me ask you: Are you Buddhist, or are you Christian?

If you put "or" there, then I have no answer. If you ask me, "Are you a Buddhist?" I would say that I am seeking to live in a way that is modeled by the Buddha, the Awakened One—with wisdom to see things as they are, and with a compassion that comes out of seeing the way things are; namely, that everything is interconnected. I'd like to be that.

Are you Christian?

I have tried to live in the way that Jesus taught us to live—to live in the love of God, and share that love with others. So if you ask me, "Are you Christian?" I would say that I would like to be, and I am doing the best I can to be worthy of that name. But if you ask me, "Are you Buddhist *and* Christian?" I would be hesitant, because that would compromise the two traditions, to suggest that they can just be mixed.

Many people I encounter in Western Buddhist sitting have rejected Christianity because they have suffered under a very punitive form of it. Some people feel wounded by the very language of the faith. Even a word like "salvation" can be painful.

Right—the hellfire and thunder and so on. "If you don't take Jesus as your savior, then you're damned forever." But if you look at that word itself, it comes from the same root as the Spanish toast ¡*salud!*, which means "to your health; well-being." In Latin, it's *salus*, and the Greek origin is *holos*, which means "whole." The wholeness that we are all longing for, that we are all meant to arrive at, is what we would correctly understand as salvation. We all need that kind of salvation.

In your experience—both in your own practice and in working with students—does something different happen in Zen meditation *in the mind* for a Christian from what happens for a Buddhist?

If we take the mind according to the Zen context, as that which leads us to what is beyond words and concepts, then I would say that whether you're a Christian or a Muslim or a Jew or an atheist or a Buddhist, what happens in Zen practice should not be different. It's an immersion in the silence and an appreciation of all that's there. And all that's there is not something we can limit through our thoughts and concepts and our restricted notions of being or nonbeing.

With a student, then, you're listening for whatever concepts they're holding on to, and inviting them to put them down?

When a student comes to me—whether Christian or Jewish or Buddhist or atheist—I just deal with the matter at hand. Now, if the student comes with questions and expressions that come from a religious background, then I try to help them use those very words to lead to the realm of mystery. A person's own worldview and background and vocabulary can be the gateway to that.

So you are trying to find out whether someone's concepts are going to be in the way, or whether they're going to be part of the path?

Yes, precisely. It's very difficult to discern, but really important, because otherwise we might also be throwing the baby out with the bathwater. If we unskillfully reject or ignore a concept or term just because it comes from a particular culture or philosophical or theological matrix, then we might be missing an opportunity to go *beyond* the concept. One needs to be very sensitive. A listening ear is really important for guiding others in walking this path.

Is the God you know now the same God you walked into Zen practice with the first time?

Over time, my sense of God would have shifted no matter what. It started happening in my mid-teens, even before I entered the Jesuits. I had this experience of sitting in a classroom, in an English literature class. I was only half-interested, and I started looking out the window, at this clear, blue, empty sky. And then it came to me: that the universe is finite, but unbounded. Suddenly the notion of God "up there," up in the sky, didn't make any sense for me. There was no place for it anymore. I felt relief, but at the same time, a sense of anxiety. What do I do if there's no such thing? How do I live my life? The notion of God that I had as a child had to die first, and the death of that God is what led me to the God that is beyond words and concepts.

In the way that emptiness is beyond words and concepts?

If you really look at what the term *shunyata* is trying to say, it's another mind-boggling thing that cannot be caged in a strict rational form. In one sense, there's *nothing* left. But you can also say that's where *everything* begins. I was doing this kind of mental gymnastics when I was preparing for ordination. Reading the Pauline letters [in the New Testament], the notion of *pleroma* [fullness] in Paul, and *ta panta en pasin*, the "all in all," caught my attention. The Greek expression struck me: fullness in a way that there's nothing more that can be filled. Ultimate fullness corresponds to emptiness.

We also call it "mystery," that which makes our mouth just shut in holy wonder. And I believe that that's what Zen opens to us, that sense of mystery, that sense of awe that what is, *is*. Form is form, and yet we know that that form is also emptiness. I'm saying nonsense here, perhaps. But that's the kind of holy nonsense that Zen comes from.

It seems that Zen is a practice of *experience* of the mystery, not talk *about* it, though it may result in some talk. The New Testament, likewise, is the words left by people who *had an experience*. They wanted to find a way to talk about that experience. But it isn't really like normal talk. Your book *Zen and the Spiritual Exercises: Paths of Awakening and Transformation* (2013) discusses this parallel.

Saint Ignatius proposed a series of meditative and very discursive exercises for examining your sinfulness, checking out your day, seeing what you did that was according to God's will and what was not—a very left-brained kind of approach to spirituality. Zen is a more direct way of inviting people to "just sit and behold in the silence." Can those two go together? For me, it is the "Contemplation on Divine Love" [the final contemplation in the Spiritual Exercises] that is the summit of the exercises. That's exactly what happens in sitting in stillness in Zen. You're simply soaked in that divine love that is beyond words, and you allow it to fill you, inundate you, and move you so that you can live a life grounded on that, offering yourself to others.

We don't usually use the word "goal" in Zen, but can you discuss how we may arrive at a kind of goal?

I would rather call it the fruit or outcome of practice. In spiritual paths in general, there seem to be three stages that have distinctive characteristics but that are related in a developmental way. First there is the stage of purification or purgation: when a person begins to receive the impulse of the infinite. In the Buddhist tradition, we call it the bodhi mind, when you begin to ask, "What is this all about?" "How can I live my life in the most authentic way?" In Zen, I would say that's the stage when one begins to realize that there's a big gap between one's True Self and where one is right now. From a Christian perspective, it might be a sense of being separated from the ultimate reality that we call God, a sense of sinfulness.

As one goes through the purification stage, one gets to a sense of illumination, where you have these insights: "Ah, I need to do this," or "That's a wonderful realization of this or that reality," and so on. The stage of illumination gives us a clearer sense of where we're heading, that we're on the right track. Then it culminates in the stage of union, where one experiences that one is not separate at all. Those three paths seem to have congruencies: purification, illumination, and union. That's what I try to map out in my book *Zen and the Spiritual Exercises*, taking Zen on the one hand and the Spiritual Exercises on the other as parallel paths of transformation.

What kind of person results from this practice?

One becomes an ordinary person, but in an extraordinary way. Your words are still there, your hang-ups may still be there, you still have to deal with all your karmic baggage and so on, but you see it in a totally different light. You're at peace with yourself, at peace with the world. Not in a complacent sense, but in the sense that you can simply devote yourself to a life of compassion. From a Christian perspective, we use the word *perfection*, but it's not that now I'm perfect. It really means living as Christ did.

Becoming Christlike?

Yes. And what does that mean? Emptying oneself—*kenosis*. This happens not in any abstract way, but in really giving yourself utterly in the service of others, so that you may be of benefit. It's like the Buddhist chant "May all beings be at ease"—there's a congruence there. I won't use the word *same*, but you can see how Christianity and Zen resonate with each other.

I think this is actually where there's the deepest point of contact, but contemporary Christianity doesn't promote it very much. Sometimes I wonder whether Zen has attracted the number of Christians it has because it's the corrective needed for the way we've been living with our Christianity.

It speaks to those who want to live authentically. The emerging church movement, where Christians are trying to live in a way that is different from the so-called institutional forms of Christianity, is an indication that those institutions are not living up to the task of providing spiritual nourishment. That calls for deeper reflection and self-critique on the part of the managers of that institutional church. There you go—you're one of them!

Yes, I'm one of them! So it seems that the use of koans in the Sanbo Zen lineage has made using traditional scriptures for teaching a natural move for you.

Oh, yes, indeed. Right now, I am looking at scriptural passages—Psalms and Proverbs and so on—to see how they might also be material for koans that can provoke an experience in the practitioner right here and now. In this way, Christians might find that Zen practice can enhance an appreciation of what was already there in the Christian Gospel. It might also invite people in Zen practice to consider that it doesn't just have to be the Buddhist vocabulary that they can use in order to go deep into Zen, but that there are other fingers pointing to the moon. These passages might lead us to a full revelation of that moon.

The Rev. Jane Lancaster Patterson, PhD, is Assistant Professor of New Testament at Seminary of the Southwest in Austin, Texas, and codirector of St. Benedict's Workshop in San Antonio, where she lives.

Acknowledgments

This book owes its existence to countless individuals I have encountered in my journey through this life, many of whose names my rapidly fading memory is not able recall, as well as some who remain in my heart for life. Conveying a lifetime of gratitude to each and all of them, here I will just name those who had a direct or indirect role in helping this book see the light of day.

It was Sister Pascaline Coff, OSB, founder and administrator for over three decades of the Osage Monastery of the Benedictine Sisters of Perpetual Adoration in Sand Springs, Oklahoma, who first invited me to offer guided Zen retreats for the community of sisters there and for a wider circle of friends of the monastery. The monastery was inspired by the vision of Father Bede Griffiths, OSB, for a spiritual center and community open to all seekers, and who thus founded such a community, called Shantivanam Ashram, in India. This initial invitation in Spring 1990 somehow led to a habit-forming pattern, so from 1990 until 2009, every spring (March or April) I would fly (or sometimes drive) to Sand Springs from our home in Dallas to conduct five- or six-day Zen retreats at the monastery.

For practically all of those retreats Helen A. Cortes, now my co-teacher at Maria Kannon Zen Center, served as the liaison with the monastery as well as organizer of those retreats, sending out announcements and communicating with prospective participants. Helen also assisted in the role of monitor (timekeeper, schedule coordinator, audio recorder, photographer) during those retreats. And she also found time to sit and join in the silence as a practitioner herself. Without her foresight of having the talks delivered during those retreats to be put on audio recording, this book would not have come to be.

To all the Benedictine sisters of the Osage Monastery beginning with Sister Pascaline, and including Sister Priscilla, the late Sister Helen Barrow (the Hermit Sister), Sisters Joretta, Benita, Kathleen, Sarah, and several others, and also the Benedictine Oblates and other lay supporters, and the wider circle of friends who had participated in those Zen retreats at the monastery through the years, I convey my heartfelt thanks. Deep gratitude to Bob Doenges, who gave a very generous gift that allowed Osage Monastery to continue in operation as the Osage Forest of Peace after the Benedictine Sisters had decided to move on from Sand Springs. Special thanks also to Elaine Dishman, John Douglas, Amy Garrett, Jon Hart, John Ockels, and Father Brian Pierce, OP, who served on the board and kept the Forest open and available as a place of spiritual nourishment open to all for a number of years, with Sister Jane Comerford as resident director. I thank and also congratulate the current board members, Shirley Cox, JoAnn Huber, Joli Jensen, Gaye Mazzei, Jim Mazzei, Kathy Payne, and Susan Singh, for carrying the torch, and who through their creativity and dedicated team effort, have succeeded in enabling the Forest to continue even now to be a spiritual oasis and source of nourishment for so many seekers. I thank Rev. Don Chatfield, executive director, with Karen Chatfield, Maryann Greenwald, and Sheila Lazer, who currently serve as staff members.

I also am grateful to all those who have sat and continue to sit with me in Zen practice at Maria Kannon Center in Dallas, Texas, through the years, most especially my fellow Zen teachers, Helen A. Cortes, Valerie Forstman, Maria Reis Habito, and

Senior Dharma Teacher Joe Benenate. All the persons with whom I have been privileged to sit together in this practice of Zen have been and are my teachers from whom I have learned so much.

I thank the Rev. Celia (Kitchens) Halfacre, senior pastor at Lakehills United Methodist Church, Lakehills, Texas, who as a Master of Divinity student at Perkins School of Theology, agreed to serve as my research assistant, taking on the task of transcribing tapes of some of the talks given at the Zen retreats at Osage Monastery. Her transcriptions became the initial rough draft of this book. Angela Cenzon, Robert Cenzon, Helen A. Cortes, and Florian Habito also helped in transcribing some of the recordings. I then edited, revised, and polished the collection of transcriptions and sought to put them in a coherent structure, coming up with what is now offered as this volume.

It was my entrance into the Society of Jesus in 1964 that launched me into a spiritual journey that continues to this day. For this, I can never repay the debt of gratitude to this august company of men, founded by our Father Ignatius of Loyola in the sixteenth century, who, moved by an experience of Divine Love, became "men for others" who have dedicated their whole lives to God in the service of their fellow human beings. Having had the privilege and great blessing of being in their fold for twenty-five years (1964–89), it has now been more than twenty-five years since I parted from their company, having married and raised two sons since then. And now, I am thrilled to be able to reconnect in a new way with this esteemed company who formed me into what I am, being invited to offer an occasional course for seminarians and students at the Jesuit-run Loyola School of Theology in Quezon City, Philippines. To all the Jesuits, beginning with my Masters of Novices, the late Fathers Miguel Casals and Charles Wolf, all my co-novices, classmates and confreres, colleagues, and mentors through the years, many current as well as former Jesuits departed or still alive, untold heartfelt and lifelong gratitude.

To the Zen Master who led me by the hand into the depths of the riches of the mystery of the world of Zen, from my first formal encounter with him in 1971 until his death in 1989, the late Yamada Kōun Rōshi, and his spouse Mrs. Kazue Yamada (d. 2014), and to all my mentors, including my Zen teachers and co-practitioners through the years in our Sanbo Zen lineage, I bow in deepest respect and gratitude.

I thank my spouse, Maria Reis Habito, now a Zen teacher in her own right, who graciously and patiently set aside her own formal Zen practice and stayed at home to take care of our two sons especially during their early years through childhood and early teens while I took off to Sand Springs and other places (in addition to our home Zendo in Dallas) for several days at a time in the course of a given year to offer guidance at Zen retreats. And I thank our now young adult sons Florian and Benjamin, who bore the brunt with their mother of their father's temporary absences during those times, and who continue to give me and Maria the irreplaceable and untold joy of being parents together, ready to always be there for them no matter what. They continue to teach me so many precious things in life, and I wish them all the blessings in their lives as they pursue the path they are called to, each in their own ways.

I am grateful to the community of Perkins School of Theology, where I have been privileged to be on the faculty since 1989, and in particular to the Perkins Scholarly Outreach Award committee, with its chair Associate Dean Evelyn Parker, her assistant, Brennan Blair, and members Dean William B. Lawrence, Dr. Tamara Lewis, and Dr. Hugo Magallanes, who approved a grant allowing me to finish work on the final draft that became this book. I also convey my special thanks to Dodee and Billy Crockett, dear friends who made a generous donation to Perkins that allowed for the construction of a Labyrinth in a central location of the school campus. This prayer Labyrinth now becomes a hallmark and an invitation toward a deeper spiritual life for the entire Perkins community, as we continue in the work of theological education of religious leaders for the present and the coming generations.

I thank the Rev. Dr. Jane Patterson, professor of New Testament at Seminary of the Southwest in Austin, Texas, and codirector of St. Benedict's Workshop in San Antonio, as well as Mary Talbot, editor of *Tricycle: The Buddhist Review*, for giving me permission to include (as the appendix) an interview article on what Christians can learn from Zen practice, titled "Other Fingers Pointing to the Moon" (*Tricycle* 23, no. 4 [Summer 2014]). I thank my dear and esteemed friend and mentor, Zen Master Norman Fischer, for permission to use his translations of the Psalms in this volume (*Opening to You: Zen Inspired Translations of the Psalms* [New York: Penguin Putnam, 2002]). Unless otherwise noted, other scriptural citations are from the New Revised Standard Version.

To Robert Ellsberg, to my editor Jim Keane, former editors who have helped me and worked with me in previous publications, including Bill Burrows and Susan Perry, to Production Coordinator Maria Angelini, and to our many friends at Orbis Books, I acknowledge my deep debt of gratitude, for their willingness to consider my work worthy of lining up in the company of the so many excellent volumes published under their aegis, and allowing it to be made accessible to a wide circle of readership.

Index

absolute nothingness, 44
acceptance, 12, 14, 17, 82, 85–86, 165
advertising, 79
agape, 154
alienation, 94–95
animals, realm of, 96
anointing, 76
Aquinas, Thomas, 53
archery, 41–43
Archimedes, 102
As Good as It Gets (dir. Brooks), 14
ashuras, 96
tman, 25
attentiveness, 50
Augustine of Hippo, 6, 7, 13–14, 91, 92, 119, 141
awakening, 7–9, 90, 96–97, 167
    experience of, 36–38
    realization of, 98–99
    search for, 39–43

Beatitudes, 117–18, 126–27, 131, 136, 139, 148–50, 158–59
beginner's mind, 37–38
being, six realms of, 94–99
be-ing, 111, 112–13, 160–63
Being Peace (Thich Nhat Hanh), 58–59
believing, linked with seeing, 35–36
Benton, Robert, 74
Bible, Zen practice and, 169, 170–71. *See also* Matthew 5; Matthew 13; Psalm 42; Psalm 46
Big Mind, 149

binaries, 44–45. *See also* dualistic thinking
blessedness, 117–20, 124–28, 142–43, 149–52, 154, 163. *See also* Beatitudes
bliss, 25–26
Bodhidharma, 7
bodhi mind, 98, 180
Brahman, 25
Brahma-vihāra, 26–31
Brantschen, Niklaus, 71
breathing, 9, 31, 38, 99
    archery and, 41–43
    attentive, 49, 82
    connected to life, 49–50
    guidelines for, 83, 122, 124
    listening during, 55–56
    as Mysterious Event, 85
    practice of, 36
    and unraveling life's mystery, 49–50
Buddha, 36, 90
Buddha, the, 7–8. *See also* Siddhartha Gautama
Buddhahood, 90–91, 96–97
"Burnt Norton" (Eliot), 102–3
busyness, 110–11

Capra, Fritjof, 156
Chan/Zen, in China, 6–7
Christ, 106, 181
Christianity, language of, 176
Christian spirituality, 132
co-creators, 63

Coff, Pascaline, x
community, 8–9, 59–63
compassion, 28–29, 32, 67–68, 77, 146, 147
conflict, cycle of, 23–24
Conjectures of a Guilty Bystander (Merton), 113–16
connectedness, 8–9. *See also* interconnectedness
conscience, 73
consciousness, 25–26, 44, 101. *See also* ego-consciousness
"Contemplation on Divine Love" (Ignatius), 179
contemplative life, 148
contemplative practice, 155–59
    dissatisfaction and, 13–14
    engaging the world, 1–2
    guidelines for, 30–31, 35
    Zen, 9. *See also* Zen practice
contentment, 63–66, 97
Cortes, Helen, 91–92
cosmology, 157
creation, goodness of, 118–19

Dao, the, 69
darkness, acceptance of, 85–86
Dazu Huike (Taiso Ega), 6–7
death, unavoidability of, 34
deification, 168
delusions, 121–22
desire, 5–6, 23, 95, 107
    for belonging, 61
    cycles of, 79–80
    dissatisfaction and, 13–14
    human condition and, 24–26
    for identification, 15
    pursuit of, 48–49
    removal of, 64, 66
deva, 97
dharma
    taking refuge in, 8
    three marks of, 11–12
dissatisfaction, 4, 5, 7–8, 13–14, 81, 107–8

diversions, 24. *See also* desire
divine dwelling, 26–31, 32, 146, 147
divinization, 168
Dogen, 109, 166
dualistic thinking, 29, 30, 44–46, 61

earth community, woundedness of, 61
ego-consciousness, 102, 122
ego-delusion, 37, 98, 99, 116
Eliot, T. S., 102–3, 104
emperor, reverence for, in Japan, 51–52
emptiness, 64, 100–104, 178–79
enlightenment, 27–28, 81, 103
    experience of, 36–37
    guidance toward, 33–35
    world of, 100–101
equanimity, 30, 32, 34, 146–47
eschatology, realized, 87
Eucharist, 74–75
evangelical poverty, 131–32
evil, 73

fear, 10–19, 32
fighting (malignant) spirits, realm of, 95–96
Fischer, Norman, 15, 50
form, emptiness and, 100–104
four immeasurables, 26–30, 32, 146–47
Four Quartets (Eliot), 104
Francis of Assisi, 63
freedom, 99–100, 113, 133
fulcrum, image of, 101–2

Gateless Gate, 69–70, 133–34
goals, working toward, 180
God. *See also* Holy One
    acknowledgment of, 18–19
    blessings of, 117–21
    compassion of, 67–68
    as creator, 118–19
    goodness of, 152
    kin-dom of, 88, 105

love of, 155
mystery of, 157, 159–60, 168
name of, 118. *See also* Holy One;
  YHWH
presence of, 91, 92
as pure be-ing, 160–62
reign of, 139–42. *See also* kin-dom
  of God
seeing, 35–36
understanding of, 25, 178
wrestling with, 16, 17
Gonzaga, Aloysius, 137–38
Good Samaritan, 127
goodness, 67, 77
grace, xiv, 43, 46, 67–68, 76,
  77, 99–100, 116
gratitude, 125, 126
Great Resolve, 81
Ground of Being, 160

Habito, Ruben L. F., interview with,
  172–82
Hakuin, 89–90. *See also* Song of
  Zazen
Hand, Thomas, 164, 174
Hardy, Thomas, 68
*Healing Breath: Zen for Christians
  and Buddhists in a Wounded
  World* (Habito), 173
Heart Sutra, 100–102
heaven. *See also* kin-dom of heaven
  depiction of, 144–45
  meaning of, 141
heavenly beings, realm of, 97
Heidegger, Martin, 45
hell
  depiction of, 144
  as other people, 95
  as state of life, 94
hell-dwellers, 94
Herrigel, Eugen, 41
hierarchy of beings, contemplation of, 157–58
Hinduism, 25
Holy One

name of, 51–53
revelation of, 52
hope, 74
Hopkins, Gerard Manley, 85
human beings
  blessedness of, 119–21. *See also*
    Beatitudes
  depravity of, 119
  existential situation of, 96–97
  realm of, 96–97
  tragedies in lives of, 109–10
human condition, 24–26
hungry ghosts, realm of, 95

"I AM," 17–19, 53, 55–68, 73, 76,
  78, 104, 162–66, 168
Ignatius of Loyola, x, 155–58, 179
illumination, 180
immersion trips, 128–30
impermanence, 11–13, 108, 109
infinite, longing for, 25–26
interconnectedness, 17, 28–30, 55,
  59–63, 64–65, 67, 87, 88, 90,
  104, 142, 148, 156–57, 176
Introduction to Metaphysics
  (Heidegger), 45
Isasi-Díaz, Ada María, 88, 142
Israelites, as chosen people,. 118

Japan, reverence in, for the emperor,
  51–52
Jesus, xiii, 165
  dwelling of, 33
  parables of, as koans, 173
  spirit of, 131
  spiritual retreats of, xii–xiii
  transfiguration of, 112
Joshu, 39, 69–71, 85
joy, 29–30, 32, 146–47
just sitting, 37, 83–84, 116. *See also*
  sitting

Kapleau, Philip, 40–41
karuna, 28–29
kenosis, 181

kensho, 36, 84
kin-dom of God (kin-dom of heaven), 75, 87–88, 105, 137, 142–43
    manifestation of, 147
    participation in, 145–48
kingdom of heaven, 79, 141
kinship, 27–28, 29
koans, 38–40, 69–72, 84–86, 103, 124, 133–37, 172, 173, 174, 182
Kyoto School, 44

Linji Zen, 38
lion and lamb, living peacefully, 68, 75
living water, 20, 26, 30, 32, 65, 159, 163, 166
Living Zen, Loving God (Habito), 173
Lord's Prayer, 141
Lotus Sutra, 93
love
    presupposing communion, 155
    seeking of, 77–78
    unconditional, 158
loving-kindness, 27–28, 30, 32, 146, 147
Luke, message of, 127
Luther, Martin, 119

Maclean, Norman, 20
Magnificat, 127, 137
Mahāyāna Buddhism, 93, 100
Maria Kannon Zen Center (Dallas, TX), 172, 173
Mary (mother of Jesus), 127, 132, 137
material goods, desire for, 4–6
Matthew, Gospel of
    chapter 5, 117–18, 126–27, 131, 136, 139, 148–50, 158–59
    chapter 13, 79, 85, 86, 88–89
meditation, 47, 99, 124
meditative practice, 35
mercy, 67
Merton, Thomas, 113–15
metanoia, xiii, 19, 29, 139–40

mettā, 27, 147
mind, calming of, 49, 50, 82, 83
Moses, revelation to, 52–53, 56–57, 162
muditha, 29–30
Mu koan, 39–40, 84–85, 86, 173
Mumokan, 133–34
Mumon (Wumen), 134–35
mystery
    experience of, 179
    of God, 157, 159–60, 168
    science and, 156–57
    source of, 152

Nansen, 70–71
Net of Indra, 87
New Testament, 76, 94, 131, 179.
    See also Matthew, Gospel of
Nishitani, Keiji, 44–46
nonattachment, 132–33, 140
nothingness, 44, 137
not-self, 11

ordinary mind, 70
original sin, 119–20, 168

parable of the prodigal son, 94
parable of the treasures.
    See Matthew 13
peace
    gift of, 2, 17
    place of, 2, 4, 17, 46, 73, 77, 146
    seeking of, 17
    source of, 63
pearl of great price, 88–89, 90, 108
personal history, examining, 123
Places in the Heart (dir. Benton), 74–75
"Please Call Me by My True Names" (Thich Nhat Hanh), 57–59
poor in spirit, 128–36, 139, 140
posture, 49, 82, 99
poverty, vow of, 132–33
power, drive for, 5–6

powerlessness, 3–4, 5, 43
Psalm 23, 50–51, 55–56, 66–69,
    72–74, 76–78. *See also* I AM
Psalm 42, 20–22
Psalm 46, 2–3, 6–7, 9–10, 15–20,
    22, 26, 32–33, 46, 171
pure of heart, 159–61, 166–68
purification, 180

realized eschatology, 87
Redford, Robert, 20
refuge
    place of, 32
    seeking of, 3–4, 7–9, 18
refugees, 4
reign of God, 142. *See also* kin-dom
    of God
Reis, Maria, 172–73
relationship, 28
relaxed attentiveness, xiv
Religion and Nothingness (*Shūkyō to
    wa Nanika*; Nishitani), 44–46
rest, place of, 2, 4, 7
restlessness, 4, 6–7
retreats. *See* spiritual retreat
righteousness, 69, 72
Rinzai Zen, 38, 89
A River Runs through It (dir. Redford),
    20
Ryōanji, 63–64

salvation, 170, 176
samsara, 98
Sanbo Zen, 172, 174, 182
sangha, 8–9, 59, 60
Sartre, Jean-Paul, 107
science, 156–57
Second Chan (Zen) Ancestor, 6–7
security, letting go of, 11
self
    acceptance of, 165
    as Buddha, 90
    construction of, 15
    identification of, 53–55, 70
    letting go of, 31

wrestling with, 16–17
self-pride, 121–22
self-satisfaction, 5
self-worth, mistaken sense of, 121–22
Serenity Prayer, 147
sesshin, xiii
Seven-Storey Mountain, The (Merton),
    116
Shakyamuni Buddha, 33, 109, 133
shikantaza, 37
shunyata, 178
Siddhartha Gautama, 6–7, 81
sin. *See* original sin
sitting, 37. *See also* just sitting
    guidelines for, 83
    meditative, 84, 124
    in stillness, 23, 53, 55, 65, 125–26
six worlds, 94–99
Song of Zazen (Hakuin), 89–90,
    92–93, 97–99
Soto tradition, 37
spiritual books, 24
spiritual community, 59–63
Spiritual Exercises (Ignatius), x,
    154–55, 172, 174, 179, 180
spiritual life, looking at the world, 2
spiritual practice
    health and, 89
    outcomes of, 180–81
spiritual retreats, xii–xiii, 80, 87
Sri Ramana Maharshi, 109
standpoint of emptiness, 45–46
Steindl-Rast, David, 125
stillness, 46. *See also* peace
    experience of, 17–19, 22, 26, 29
    guidelines for, 83
    inner, 49, 50
    listening in, 99
    nourishment and, 68–69
    sitting in, 23, 53, 55, 65, 125–26
still waters, 68
suffering, 28–29, 30, 57
śūnyatā, 101
surrender, 17, 28, 31, 43, 80–81
"*Suscipe*" (Ignatius), 155

Suzuki, Shunryu, 31, 36, 37–38
sympathetic joy, 146–47

Tao of Physics, The (Capra), 156
theosis, 168
Thich Nhat Hanh, 57–59
thirst, inner, 20–24, 26, 50
Three Jewels, 7
Three Marks of Dharma, 11
Three Pillars of Zen, The (ed.
        Kapleau), 40–41
Tillich, Paul, 160, Paul, 167
*To Shine One Corner of the World:
        Moments with Shunryu Suzuki*
        (Chadwick et al.), 31, 36
Toy Story (dir. Lasseter), 104
transformation, 37. See also *metanoia*
treasure, 83–84, 86
    awakening to, 111–12
    claiming of, 81, 82
    expectation of, 92
    manifestation of, 82
    people endowed with, 64
    seeking, 86, 105–6
    source of, 94
Treatise on Loving-kindness
        (*Mettā Sutta*), 27
true nature, seeing, 36–37
True Self, 15, 36, 37, 70, 104,
        149, 166, 167, 180
trust, 10–11, 13

ultimate reality, 25
universe
    creation of, 118
    gift of, 62
upekkha, 30

walking, 12–13, 84
water
    living, 26

still, 68
Way, the, 69–70
    embodiment of, 71–72
    guidance for, 73
    realization of, 65–66
Way Is in You, The (Brantschen), 71
Wesley, John, 62
workaholism, 110

Yamada Kōun Rōshi, ix, 165–66,
        170, 172, 174–75
Yasutani Hakuun Rōshi, 40, 175
YHWH, 118
    meaning of, 52–53
    as sacred term, 51–52

Zen and the Art of Archery
        (Herrigel), 41–43
Zen Buddhism, xiii, 6–7
    Christians' practice of, 175–82
    contemplative practice and, 9
    curiosity about, 47–48
    experience of, 170
    guidance in, 47–48, 55
    practice of, 47–50, 55, 82–83,
        169–71, 177, 179–81
    retreats and, xiii–xiv, 111, 112,
        121, 124
Zen chores, 111, 112–13
Zen Mind, Beginner's Mind
        (Suzuki), 36
Zen practice, 116, 122, 164
Zen retreats, 111, 112, 121, 124
*Zen and the Spiritual Exercises: Paths
        of Awakening and Transformation*
        (Habito), 179, 180
Zen talks, 149, 159
zero, function of, 101
zero-point, 137